Also available from the
8 Keys to Mental Health Series

8 Keys to Stress Management
Mark Bowers

8 Keys to Eliminating Passive-Aggressiveness
Andrea Brandt

8 Keys to Forgiveness
Robert Enright

8 Keys to Recovery from an Eating Disorder:
Effective Strategies from Therapeutic Practice and Personal Experience
Carolyn Costin, Gwen Schubert Grabb

8 Keys to Parenting Children with ADHD
Cindy Goldrich

8 Keys to Building Your Best Relationships
Daniel A. Hughes

8 Keys to Practicing Mindfulness:
Practical Strategies for Emotional Health and Well-Being
Manuela Mischke Reeds

8 Keys to Trauma and Addiction Recovery
Lisa M. Najavits

8 Keys to Safe Trauma Recovery:
Take-Charge Strategies to Empower Your Healing
Babette Rothschild

8 Keys to Br
Rob

8 Keys to Str
Elizabeth.

8 Keys to End Bullying:
Strategies for Parents & Schools
Signe Whitson

8 Keys to Mental Health Series
Babette Rothschild, Series Editor

The 8 Keys series of books provides consumers with brief, inexpensive, and high-quality self-help books on a variety of topics in mental health. Each volume is written by an expert in the field, someone who is capable of presenting evidence-based information in a concise and clear way. These books stand out by offering consumers cutting-edge, relevant theory in easily digestible portions, written in an accessible style. The tone is respectful of the reader and the messages are immediately applicable. Filled with exercises and practical strategies, these books empower readers to help themselves.

8 KEYS TO OLD-SCHOOL PARENTING FOR MODERN-DAY FAMILIES

MICHAEL MASCOLO

Foreword by Babette Rothschild

W. W Norton & Company

New York • London

For information about permission to reproduce selections from this book, write to
Permissions, W. W. Norton & Company, Inc., 500 Fifth Avenue, New York, NY 10110

For information about special discounts for bulk purchases,
please contact W. W. Norton
Special Sales at specialsales@wwnorton.com or 800-233-4830

Manufacturing by Quad Graphics, Fairfield
Production manager: Leeann Graham

Library of Congress Cataloging-in-Publication Data

Mascolo, Michael F.
    8 keys to old school parenting for modern-day families / Michael
Mascolo ; foreword by Babette Rothschild. — First edition.
        pages cm. — (8 keys to mental health series)
    Includes bibliographical references and index.
    ISBN 978-0-393-70936-0 (pbk.)
    1. Parenting. 2. Parent and child. I. Title. II. Title: Eight keys
to old school parenting for modern-day families.
    HQ755.8.M359   2015
    306.874—dc23
            2014036569

ISBN: 978-0-393-70936-0 (pbk.)

W. W. Norton & Company, Inc., 500 Fifth Avenue, New York, N.Y. 10110
www.wwnorton.com
W. W. Norton & Company Ltd., Castle House, 75/76 Wells Street,
London W1T 3QT

1 2 3 4 5 6 7 8 9 0

To Alicia, Seth, Mica and Jake

Contents

Acknowledgments

In preparing this book, I have benefitted greatly from the assistance and support of many people. Without the help of Kurt Fischer, Michael Basseches and the late James Mancuso, I could never have developed the ideas and perspectives on which this book is based. Jin Li convinced me of the importance of the idea of moral self-cultivation. Christina Hardway was always sitting on my shoulder, helping me to understand the importance of seeing both the good and bad in any historical epoch. Thank you to Suzanne Provencher for seven years of collaboration on our parenting newspaper, which allowed me to forge many of the ideas contained in this book. My deep appreciation to Alex and Jenise Aminoff for their openness, proactivity, intelligence and support, and to Trish Pini for being the quintessential cheerleader and connector. Thank you to Deborah Malmud for her for creativity and her confidence in me, and to Babette Rothschild for her words of wisdom. Thank you to Seth and Jake for teaching me at least as much as I try to teach to you. I thank my wife, Alicia Diozzi, for always telling me what she thought, for working to deliver me from academic writing, for her keen proofreader's eye, and for her unrelenting emotional support. I have drawn on the ideas of many people in this book; the responsibility for any errors or misrepresentations that might have ensued from my use of these ideas is mine.

Foreword

Babette Rothschild, Series Editor

Parents have always struggled with how best to help their children grow and guide them towards being productive adults who fit well into their families, workplaces, neighborhoods, and cultures. Through many centuries, parenting in most cultures has been based on a rigid set of values, "my way or the highway," sort of thinking. This is how most of our ancestors were raised. The children were expected to conform to the rules and behaviors with tough (often physical) punishments for any and all infractions.

At the turn of the 20th century, Freud's psychoanalysis and psychology became influential in child rearing. The modern view was that the traditional parenting and upbringing methods might be to blame for psychological distress and other problems in adulthood. Parents became concerned about how their children would fare psychologically throughout life. It became a popular practice to prioritize easing a child's stress and to consider the child's feelings about rules and punishments, putting the child at the center of the parenting. In the extreme, children were making their own decisions about what was and was not acceptable, sometimes virtually raising themselves. This approach spared parents the risk of making mistakes, but also deprived those children of much needed guidance and containment.

This "child-centric" trend reached into the schools. I remember in the 1960s the emergence of *free schools* that had many of the same values of child-centered parenting. Children were encouraged to be self-directing, which sometimes produced high achievement, but for many children was a disaster because of the lack of boundaries and limits. This kind of free-school teaching trend has reversed in many sectors, giving way to a return to more structured teaching and guidance. Perhaps parenting needs to follow suit.

Michael Mascolo's 8 *Keys to Old School Parenting for Modern Day Families* is a breath of fresh air in the current library of parenting literature. He takes a critical look at the recent trends toward child-centered parenting, evaluating the successes and failures of that popular approach. Finding that the disadvantages have outweighed the advantages, Mascolo proposes a return to old-school values in parenting, but without the rigidity and sometimes violence of "the good-old days." He is not swinging the pendulum back to 1800s parenting, rather identifying the most important and successful features from the old school and giving them a modern twist. His is not a, "because I said so," approach, but parenting that acknowledges the need for children to be parented. Children *need*to be guided and taught in developing their character, and in reinforcing socially productive behavior. There is nothing wrong with this. There is value in discipline, (which, Mascolo emphasizes, is not the same thing as punishment). We must let children learn from mistakes and adversity. These are some of the messages in this important book.

The pendulum has swung so far in the direction of a child-centric parenting that terms like "helicopter parents" or "over-parenting" are common these days.

In my own work, I have observed that children of helicopter parents in particular, lack the resources and resilience needed to swing with the bumps and bruises of daily life. Though well intentioned, depriving children of the opportunity to deal with problems, hurts, and stresses while growing up, can leave them handicapped when faced with those same issues as adults. It is a "use it or lose it" situation. If you do not exercise the resources needed to manage stress and adversity, you do not strengthen those tools for use in the future.

I love it when language reflects culture and vice versa. A Scandinavian-coined term, *the curling parent*, perfectly describes a type of child-centered parenting where the parents seek to smooth the way for their children, much as a sweeper in the winter sport of curling smooths the ice ahead of the rock. This book is offering a different approach. Mascolo accomplishes his goals well with a generous variety of descriptions of parenting dilemmas and clear and direct advice on how to deal with them. He successfully guides parents in helping their children to grow, thrive, and gain positive self-esteem by first supporting the authority and esteem of the parent, and then giving common sense examples for how to shape a child's behavior and moral development. Mascolo is particularly strong on helping parents to set and maintain logical and firm boundaries and limits—something that has become increasingly difficult for parents in the child-centered age.

In the field of family therapy, the common wisdom when there is a child with emotional problems, is first to make sure that the parents are supported. The belief is that for a child to feel secure, the parents must be and feel secure. A foundational strength of Mascolo's 8 *Keys to Old School Parenting* is in his unfailing support of the parents who are reading the book and implementing his ideas. In many ways he is standing behind each parent reader, with a hand on their shoulder, telling them that they have much to offer their children, and that by providing an old-school environment, their children will have a much better chance as they move out into the world on their own.

8 KEYS TO OLD-SCHOOL PARENTING FOR MODERN-DAY FAMILIES

RECLAIMING PARENTHOOD

It's time to reverse the culture of indulgence and entitlement that pervades contemporary child rearing.

Have you noticed . . .

- parents who seem to "give in" to what their children want, even when it seems that they shouldn't?
- adults who seem to praise their children's behavior, even when children fail?
- parents who seem more act more like friends to their children than parents?
- children who seem to feel that they are entitled to good things in life, and that they don't have to work hard to get them?

Have you found that . . .

- children are given awards and trophies regardless of their performance in an activity (e.g., a sporting event, a play)?
- too many young people seem to call undue attention to themselves?
- too many children fail to say "please" or "thank you" or use their manners?
- children and young people seem to seek praise when they achieve success in even simple tasks?

Do you worry that . . .

- parents are being overprotective and sheltering their children from even the slightest of dangers?
- too many children seem to have difficulty regulating their impulses and emotions?
- adults are more likely to remove children from stressful events rather than teach children how to cope effectively with them?
- too many parents are afraid to say "no" to their children?

Do you ever feel that . . .

- you cannot get your children to do what you ask?
- no matter how much your children seem to get, that they are not grateful, or that they seem to always want more?
- you have to "walk on eggshells" around your children?
- your children are disrespectful?

If you have answered "yes" to the majority of these questions, then you are among the growing number of people who feel that something is not quite right with the way we as a nation are currently approaching the task of parenting our children. If you are feeling frustrated that your own children are showing some of these behaviors, you are by no means alone. Over the last several generations, parents have found themselves immersed in the well-intentioned idea that parenting should be child-centered rather than adult-centered. Child-centered thinking is based on the idea that children are active in their own development. As a result, it is better for parents to follow their children's lead rather than to insist that children adapt themselves to the prerogatives of the parent. From a child-centered view, too much parental direction can stifle a child's initiative, autonomy, and self-esteem. Although not altogether incorrect, this well-intentioned view is nonetheless flawed and has contributed to a series of unwanted and unintended consequences for our children. This book examines why this is the case and offers a series of concrete remedies to correct the situation.

Parenting with Attitude

David Elkind, a prominent developmental psychologist, once wrote that "parenting is an attitude." When I read this statement many years ago, I didn't quite understand it. I had a glimmer of what he meant. However, I kept thinking: What type of attitude? It can't *just* be an attitude, right? After all, a parent actually has to *do* something to raise children.

To have a "parenting attitude" is to have a set of values that defines who you are in relation to your child. Having the right attitude is a parent's home base — it's what the parent can return to when everyday and not-so-everyday issues arise between parents and children.

Here is the attitude that informs the content of this book:

> I am your parent. I'm not your friend, your playmate, your maid, or your chauffeur. You are not my equal. I am responsible for your safety and development. I am here to teach you how to be successful in the world. Why is this? Well, for one thing, I brought you into the world, or I at least chose to bring you into my world. For another, I love you and don't want anything bad to happen to you. But most important, it's because—right now, and for the most important things—I know more than you do. I know things that you need to know to be successful in the world. And yes, I have a better understanding of what's good for you than you do. Now, this doesn't mean that I'm all knowing and that I am not going to make mistakes: I am not all knowing. I'm going to make mistakes. But when I do, they will be honest mistakes, mistakes I've made because I did

what I thought was right for you in the moment. So no, I'm not perfect. Over time, I'm going to learn a lot from you about how to parent you. Over time, as you learn to be more and more successful in the world, I'm going to turn over more and more responsibility to you for doing things yourself and for doing things right. That's what growing up means. However, know this: If you fail to do the right thing, you're going to find me right there, showing you the way until you can get it right. So you see, even though it might not always seem to be so to you, I'm on your side. You are my son or daughter, and you're stuck with me. You're not going to get rid of me. I'm here to help you get what you want out of life, but to help you to do it in the right way. If it turns out that you want the wrong things, I'm here to help you turn the wrong things into right things. Why? Because I am your parent. I'm not your friend, your playmate, your maid, or your chauffeur . . .

Why We Need Old-School Parenting

North American and Western European families are enjoying unprecedented prosperity, freedom, and quality of life. We can boast many good things. We have also witnessed some dramatic changes in family life. Over the past half-century or more, we have witnessed (a) increasing levels of narcissism, self-focus, and self-entitlement among youth; (b) a decreasing sense of purpose and moral character; (c) increasing difficulties in coping and emotional regulation; and (d) poor academic work ethic and achievement.

During this same period, there have been changes in how we raise our children. In particular, although there are always exceptions, we have experienced a cultural shift from adult-centered to child-centered approaches to raising and educating our children. In the traditional adult-centered approach, the parents' interests occupy the center of family life. Parents set the rules, and children are socialized into the norms and expectations of the parents. In contrast, child-centered parenting is organized around the interests and needs of the child. Child-centered parenting evolved as an attempt to foster the development of autonomy, independence, and creativity in children. It emerged as a reaction against what was perceived as the overly authoritarian nature of adult-centered parenting.

The movement toward child-centered parenting, although well intentioned, has played a central role in fostering the trends in child development to which I already alluded. Child-centered parenting builds on the idea that children are active in their own development. This is, in fact, a fundamental truth about child development: Children *do* play an active role in their own development. However, as psychologist William Damon has noted, this is only a half-truth. The other half of the truth is that parents also play an active and indispensable role in fostering children's development. The error of the child-centered movement is believing that parenting is a kind of zero-sum game—that either the parent or the child is active, but not both at the same time. Given this way of thinking, it was easy to conclude that too much direction from parents could squelch a child's natural initiative, creativity, or autonomy. It was easy to conclude that active parenting stifles a child's autonomy.

Nothing can be further from the truth. Although children are active in their own development, they also need guidance, direction, and support from active parents. In an attempt to foster individual initiative, creativity, and self-esteem, child-centered parenting fails to hold children to high standards of moral conduct, social responsiveness, and academic motivation. By not offering consistently clear parental guidance and direction, we are producing generations of children who are less socially, morally, and academically skilled than their predecessors.

It is time to reclaim parenthood. Happily, we already know what types of parenting practices lead to optimal outcomes in children. Hundreds of studies in developmental psychology suggest that the key to optimal parenting lies in a combination of both high parental direction and loving support. This approach is called *authoritative parenting*, and it stands in contrast with authoritarian or permissive styles of parenting. Authoritative parents set high expectations and help children live up to those standards; they enforce high moral standards with loving acceptance. They promote self-control with social responsiveness; they teach children to make responsible choices within firmly established limits.

Authoritative parenting is no fad. Its positive effects on children have been well supported and have withstood the test of time. It is time to inject some old-school parenting into our modern sensibilities. This book explains in concrete detail how this can be accomplished.

Child-Centered Parenting: When Good Intentions Go Wrong

The child-centered approach to parenting was born of good intentions. It was meant to provide an alternative to the traditional adult-centered approach to parenting, which was considered to be overly authoritarian. In the adult-centered approach, parents take the lead in setting family rules, making family decisions, and enforcing maturity demands. Although there are many forms of parent-centered child rearing, they all embrace the idea that parents have legitimate authority over their children and thus should guide and direct their children's development.

Child-centered parenting emerged as a reaction against this approach. Although it had its origins in the progressive parenting movements of the 1920s and 1930s, it took hold with greater fervor after the 1960s. The child-centered approach puts the child rather than the parent at the center of decision making. From a child-centered perspective, children are not simply lumps of clay for parents to mold according to their wishes. Instead, children are active in their own development and learning. They are born ready to explore the world and learn through active discovery. The parent's job is to kindle rather than stifle a child's self-directed curiosity. Too much parental direction can squelch a child's initiative and damage her confidence and self-esteem. To borrow a phrase from proponents of child-centered education, a good parent functions more like "a guide on the side" rather than an all-knowing "sage on the stage."

Child-centered parents love their children and want to promote their autonomy, individuality, and creativity. Who could disagree with these values? The problem, however, is not these are bad values; the problem is that they are one-sided values. In a well-meaning attempt to promote self-directed cooperative children, child-centered parenting fails to provide the very direction that children need to develop these skills in the first place. The logic goes like this:

- If we want self-directed children, we should let our children direct themselves. Too much direction will squelch a child's inherent initiative and creativity.
- If we want our children to be active learners, we encourage them to explore the world and make their own discoveries. Too much direct instruction robs children of the opportunity to think deeply and make their own connections.
- If we want children to feel good about themselves, we should praise their initiative, effort, and accomplishments. We should avoid critical feedback that can diminish a child's confidence or self-esteem.
- If we want children to develop their own moral compass, we should encourage them to think for themselves about what makes something right or wrong. Different people have different beliefs about right and wrong. To take a hard stand on moral issues runs the

risk of imposing moral standards onto children, who must ultimately develop own thoughts about right and wrong.

The problem with this line of thinking is that children enter the world as incomplete beings. They are not little adults who can direct their own thinking, make responsible decisions, or make complex connections. It is true that children come into life with many surprising skills and abilities. However, children are nonetheless undeveloped beings; they need adults to help complete their development. They do not begin life as self-directed, empathetic, and moral beings; instead, they need parental direction and guidance of to *develop into* self-directed, empathetic, moral beings. By encouraging parents to relinquish their authority to foster the development of children's autonomy, the child-centered movement has resulted in many children who have failed to develop important socio-emotional, motivational, moral, and academic skills.

How Child-Centered Parenting Undermines Children's Development

Without the support and direction of active parents, child-centered parenting tends to produce a series of unintended outcomes. In particular, it tends to foster the development of self-focus and narcissism over concern for others, a tendency toward self-expression rather than emotional regulation, an orientation toward praise seeking rather than self-cultivation, and a preference for self-gratification over moral purpose. Figure I.1 shows the ways in which child-centered parenting leads to these developmental outcomes. Let's explore how this happens.[1]

---

1. It is important to keep in mind that no two parents are exactly alike. Not all parents who engage in child-centered parenting endorse all of these beliefs. Similarly, there are parents who reject child-centered parenting who may accept one or more of these beliefs.

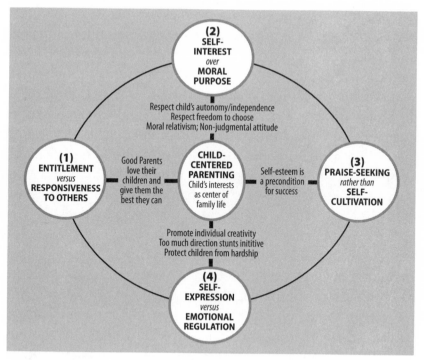

Figure I.1. The Unintended Consequences of Child-Centered Parenting

1. Child-Centered Parenting Fosters Narcissistic Entitlement over Responsiveness to Others

When we love someone, we want to take care of that person, nurture her, and give her the best that we can. We want our loved one to feel good, not bad. We want to give to our loved ones and protect them from hardship and bad experiences.

A good parent, of course, *loves* his or her children. Loving our children, we experience all of the feelings that typically occur when we love someone. We want our children to be happy. It is painful for us to see our children suffer; we want to relieve their suffering and protect them.

Love is an essential part of parenting. One of the most important things we can do for our children is to show them that we care—show them that they are loved and are thus lovable. This unshakeable sentiment is part of any healthy parent–child relationship. However, as parents we have multiple responsibilities to our children. Loving our children means nurturing them, taking care of them, and protecting them from harm. However, our primary job is to prepare our children to adapt to the challenges of life in the present and the future. Teaching children to face life's challenges involves preparing them to deal with conflict, hardship, and struggle. It requires that we do what we believe is good for children, regardless of whether our children think or feel it is good. Although we do not like to see our children suffer, hardship is an inevitable part of life. It is essential to teach children to adapt to hardship.

Sometimes, parents express their love through a single-minded effort to make their children feel happy. Parents do this in many ways—by honoring their requests, being available to when children call, managing everyday tasks so that they are not too onerous; allowing children to make choices about things that are important to them; protecting them from strong negative emotions such as shame, guilt, embarrassment; and so forth. Doing things that make our children happy is a way of loving them. It makes parents feel good. We may even think that it makes our children love us back.

The negative effects of indulgence. However, there is a word for the single-minded attempt to make children feel happy: *indulgence*. When we cater to a child's whims, we teach the child that what he wants is more important that what other people want and more important than what *we* want! This produces children who are entitled and self-absorbed (formerly called "brats"). A child who is indulged comes to think primarily of his own needs. This is because he has rarely been required to take the needs of others into consideration. As a result, an indulged child comes to think of himself as special and as entitled to have his needs met. He does not learn to be responsive to the needs of others.

According to psychologist Jean Twenge, over the past decades, young people have become increasing more self-absorbed, concerned with their own desires and needs, and more focused on their own rights and concerns.[2] Between 1980 and 2006, scores on the Narcissism Personality Inventory have increased steadily among college students. This inventory allows a researcher to estimate the extent to which people express behaviors reflecting an attitude of authority, superiority, entitlement, vanity, exploitation, exhibitionism, and self-sufficiency. Changes in narcissism over the past 25 years are unprecedented and quite real. In the span of a generation, something significant has happened to alter the moral focus on young people.

We might think that "giving children what they want" will make them happy. When we imagine a loving relationship with our children, we may imagine a state of bliss. Out of love, we give to our children and experience the pleasure of their happiness. They come to appreciate our giving and love us in return. However, that's not what happens. More typically, indulgent parenting breeds chaos. Children who are indulged develop a sense of entitlement. As a result, they place high demands on parents and express little gratitude. This puts the parent in a trap. Frustrated with their children's ungrateful demands, parents shift between indulging children further (giving children what they want to placate them) or becoming angry and controlling (scolding their children out of anger and frustration). In this way, the parent who indulges the child out of love produces the *opposite* of what they set out to accomplish.

2. Child-Centered Parenting Promotes the Development of Self-Interest over Moral Purpose

Americans have always had an ambivalent feelings toward authority. After all, the United States was founded on the prin-

2. Twenge, J. M., Konrath, S., Foster, J. D., Keith Campbell, W. W., & Bushman, B. J. (2008). Egos inflating over time: A cross-temporal meta-analysis of the Narcissistic Personality Inventory. *Journal of Personality*, 76(4), 875–902.
Twenge, J. M., Konrath, S., Foster, J. D., Campbell, W., & Bushman, B. J. (2008). Further evidence of an increase in narcissism among college students. *Journal of Personality*, 76(4), 919–928.

ciple of freedom from arbitrary authority. The founding fathers wanted to break free from what they took to be the arbitrary authority of the British Crown. American citizens are self-determining individuals with rights that cannot be violated by government or other citizens. These rights to life, liberty, and the pursuit of happiness are inscribed in the Declaration of Independence and continue to structure American life to this very day.

Given its importance, it is not surprising that Americans would want to promote the values of personal autonomy, independence, and self-determination in their family lives. The child-centered approach to parenting reflects these values. Parents who adopt a child-centered approach often view their children as individuals with rights that must be respected. These include the right to self-determination (autonomy), the right to make one's own choices (when ready), as well as rights to privacy, property, and so forth. In an attempt to respect the rights of individual children, child-centered parents tend to elevate children to the status of equals or near equals. Treating children more or less as equals, however, comes at the expense of a parent's authority. The idea that children should have a say in choices that affect them puts limits on the parent's authority.

As a result, when it comes to issues of morality, child-centered parents can become a bit squeamish. By valuing the autonomy of individuals, child-centered parents are reluctant to impose their moral values on others. When dealing with children, child-centered parents tend to believe that rather than imparting a fixed system of morals onto the child, it is better to try to help children discover their own sense of morality. In the spirit of self-determination, children should not be taught *what* to think; instead, parents should help children learn *how* to think for themselves.

For many parents, teaching children how to think becomes especially important within the global world. As technology makes it easier to communicate around the globe, it becomes increasingly clear that people differ in their views of right and wrong. What one person takes to be "right" might be "wrong" from the perspective of another. So, for many parents, there is no single "correct" set of moral rules that can be applied to everyone. This tends to make parents pause before expressing their moral values in public, and also makes them reluctant make strong claims about right and wrong to their children. Behaviors become "inappropriate" and "not okay" rather than "right" or "wrong." Rather than imposing one's morality onto one's children, parents support children in their attempts to find their own ways.

The central need for parental authority. The problem with being a "guide on the side" when it comes to moral development is that children are simply not very good at creating moral solutions to everyday problems. A six-year-old in the throes of a dispute with a sibling over a toy is not in a position to conjure up inventive ways of resolving the dispute. Even if she were, she would be poor at putting her solution into action. Besides, moral behavior is not so much a matter of putting rational thinking into action (e.g., "You take half and I'll take half") as it is a matter of experiencing moral feeling. Doing the right thing often requires cultivating feelings of empathy, sympathy, and compassion for others. Furthermore, avoiding doing the wrong thing is often a matter of experiencing difficult emotions, including feelings of guilt, shame, embarrassment, and even fear. Protecting children from such feelings is tantamount to inviting wrongdoing. Such moral emotions arise when parents are active in enforcing moral standards. They are not experiences that develop on their own.

The idea that I should not impose my moral beliefs on you is something that is most relevant to interactions among adults. Adults are equals as they attempt to convince each other about the pros and cons of any given issue. However, there is danger in extending this line of thinking to relations between parents and children. Parents and children are *not* equals. Parents have legitimate authority over their children. Parents gain their authority in at least two ways. First, parental authority is legitimized by the fact that parents tend to know more than their children and thus are more competent than their children. Second, and more important, parental authority is legitimized by the fact that parents are responsible for their children's development and well-being. Thus, parents not only have a right to exert authority over their children, it is their *responsibility* to do so. To fail to do so is to fail to fulfill one's responsibility as a parent.[3]

Without proactive guidance from parents, child-centered attempts to foster self-direction in moral decision-making are likely to fail. Instead of learning to be responsive to others, children are more likely to learn to act on the basis of self-interest—especially if parents fall into the trap of mistaking indulgence for love.

The role of parents in promoting a moral sense of purpose. Parents are the most important sources of their children's moral development. For this reason, parents should not be afraid to articulate their moral beliefs and hold children to high standards. A partial list of virtues is provided in the Circle of Virtues that appears in Figure I.2.

Perhaps the most important gift we can give our children is helping them gain a sense of who they are and who they want to be. This long developmental process begins when children are very young but does not come to fruition until adolescence and young adulthood. A child's sense of purpose comes from the thousands of interactions that she has with parents, teachers, and peers, especially those who have a strong evaluative or moral aspect to them. Who am I? What type of person do I want to be? What type of person should I become?

---

3. In placing conditions on the legitimacy of parental authority, it follows that a parent's authority over his or her children would be delegitimized if he or she were unable to fulfill his or her responsibilties as parent. Thus, if, for some reason, the child's knowledge or competence were superior to the adults (which often occurs, for example, when the discussion turns to electronic media), then the parent ceases to have authority over that particular aspect of life. Second, to the extent that a parent fails to demonstrate the capacity to assume responsibility for a child's development and well-being, the parent's authority loses its moral basis.

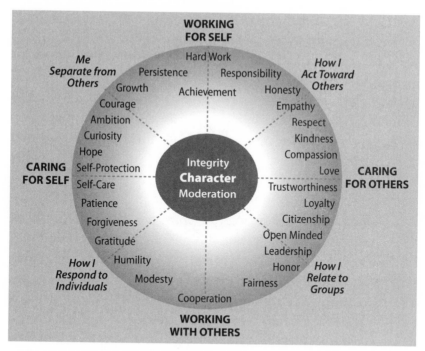

Figure I.2. The Circle of Virtues

A child's sense of purpose—his or her identity—is a kind of stance. It is a kind of position in relation to the world. It says, "This is who I am; this is what I stand for." As a kind of stance, a peson's identity or sense of purpose is something that is organized by values. Because parents are such an important source of a child's values, parents can play an indispensable role in assisting a child in developing a sense of purpose in life. As children grow older—and especially as they pass through adolescence—parents can address such questions explicitly. Who do you want to become? What role will school, family, social life, sports, community play in your life? Who are your role models, that is, whom do you respect most in your life? Whom do you respect the least? What can you do to be more like those who are worthy of admiration and respect?

Every child must eventually answer these questions for him- or herself. However, to say that children must answer these questions for themselves does not mean that children must answer these questions by themselves. Children and adolescents need the benefit of their parent's values and beliefs in their quest to create a sense of who they want to be. Parental guidance is essential from preschool through high school and beyond.

3. Child-Centered Parenting Promotes Praise-Seeking Rather than Long-Term Self-Cultivation

American parents bestow a lot of praise on their children. We do so out of the mistaken belief that self-esteem is a prerequisite for success in any given activity. The theme song for *Arthur* states this quite succinctly: "Believe in yourself, 'cause that's the place to start!" Parents and educators have taken this message to heart. If success starts with believing in ourselves, then it is necessary to praise children's abilities. Telling children how special and smart they are will make them feel good about themselves. It will give them self-esteem. Self-esteem makes children believe in themselves; believing that one can do something is a prerequisite for trying hard and succeeding.

The problem with this view is that the relationship between success and self-esteem is almost exactly the opposite of the ideas expressed in this message. We don't first gain self-esteem and then put our beliefs in ourselves into action. Instead, we attain success in our actions and, in light of our success, feel a sense of self-esteem or confidence. Our belief that we are able to perform a task—and perform it well—comes from the success that we are able to achieve at a task.

A few moments of reflection reveals why this must be the case. Imagine that you know nothing about how to fly an airplane. Suppose that I asked you to fly an important person to the White House. You might say, "I can't do that. I don't know how." Now imagine further that I said, "Come on! Believe in yourself!" A person cannot simply believe his way into doing something that he doesn't know how to do. He needs to be shown or taught how to do it.

This leads to a second point: We can't build self-esteem on our own because we learn to be successful at novel activities by ourselves. Children need sensitive, nurturing, and challenging adults to show them how to be successful, how to do the task right, how to manage their emotions when they fail, and how to continue to work hard to improve bit by bit. This also requires that we give children corrective feedback when we teach them how to do something. Children are resilient. A child's self-esteem will not be damaged when we correct their actions. A child who feels supported and assisted en route to mastering a difficult skill will not only come to feel empowered and confident, she will also learn that the adults in her life are helpful rather than harmful.

Promoting lifelong self-cultivation. Our penchant for indiscriminant praise has deeply unwanted consequences for children and adults alike. Psychologist Carol Dweck[4] shows that praising children's abilities and achievements tends to undermine rather than strengthen a child's motivation to learn. It does this by affecting how people think about the meaning of success and failure in their lives.

When we praise a child for his ability or achievement (e.g., "Good job, Todd!"; "What a smart girl, Liz!"), we teach children that their self-esteem depends on their ability to do particular tasks: "Success at a task means that I have high ability, which makes me feel good about myself; failure means I have low ability, and I feel bad." Dweck shows the importance of

---

4. Dweck, C. (2006). *Mindset*. Random House.

Rattan, A., Savani, K., Naidu, N. R., & Dweck, C. S. (2012). Can everyone become highly intelligent? Cultural differences in and societal consequences of beliefs about the universal potential for intelligence. *Journal Of Personality And Social Psychology, 103*(5), 787–803

Yeager, D., & Dweck, C. S. (2012). Mindsets that promote resilience: When students believe that personal characteristics can be developed. *Educational Psychologist, 47*(4), 302–314

focusing not on ability but on how effort and perseverance produce gradual learning over time. Instead of praising children for being able to achieve a particular outcome (getting a hit in the baseball game), it is more important to focus on working hard and slowly cultivating new skills over time. Praising ability and task success undermines motivation because it tells children that to feel good about themselves, they must have high ability. Helping children focus on the gradual development of new skills promotes motivation by linking the child's self-concept to successive steps to mastery of a skill.

People differ in how they think about success and failure. Some people hold what Dweck calls a *fixed mindset*; others draw on a *growth mindset*. A person who has a fixed mindset believes that his or her intelligence and abilities are fixed and unchangeable: a person is born with only a certain amount of ability, and there is not much one can do to change it. A person who holds a growth mindset thinks just the opposite. Our intelligence and abilities are not fixed; they are changeable through perseverance and hard work. The fixed mindset develops when adults praise children for their ability or for their success in particular tasks. Parents perpetuate a growth mindset when they focus more on the importance of gradual learning over time, rather than showing high or low ability. These differences deeply affect how people learn. Here's how: Imagine that Bob is playing baseball at school. He has a fixed mindset and believes that he has only so much baseball ability. If he does well in the game, he is praised. He feels good about his superior baseball skills. If he does poorly, he feels badly about his low level of ability. If Bob feels that his ability is unchangeable, he is unlikely to devote the time and effort to improving his game. Believing "I am bad at baseball," he will either avoid playing altogether or only play under less challenging circumstances where he knows he can perform well. As a result, Bob never improves his baseball skill.

Miranda, however, does not believe that her abilities are fixed. She understands that if she works hard and perseveres, she can improve. Imagine that Miranda gets a hit. Rather than showing effusive praise, her coach says, "Nice swing. Now, if you hold the bat like this, and keep your eye on the ball, you'll be able to hit it even further." In this situation, Miranda is being taught that although her success is good, it is not the most important thing. What is more important is to find ways to improve one's skill through perseverance. The same logic applies if Miranda were to strike out each time at bat. If she believed that her failure was the result of having poor ability, she might feel shame. However, if she believes that success comes from perseverance, she will link her failure to not yet having learned the skill. This type of thinking develops when adults focus on the importance of perseverance rather than ability. Her coach might say, "You did well keeping your eye on the ball. I've noticed you are holding the bat way down here and swinging too early. Practice like this and let's see what happens."

Bob and Miranda have different understanding of what it means to fail. Drawing on a fixed mindset, Bob thinks that failure means he lacks ability. Based on her growth mindset, Miranda interprets failure as an indication that she needs more work to master her skill. Bob is focused on the praise and good feelings that come from showing others that he has high ability. Miranda is focused on what she has to do to learn a new skill. As a result, Bob learns to avoid challenging tasks—he might fail. In contrast, Miranda learns to embrace challenging tasks— she is sure to learn.

4. Child-Centered Parenting Promotes Self-Expression over Emotional Control and Coping

A variety of studies have demonstrated increases in behavior and emotional problems among youths over the past half-century or more. These include so-called externalizing problems, such as acting out, aggression, and difficulties with emotional control, as well as internalizing problems, such as anxiety and depression. These trends are not specific to Americans, and their causes are not entirely clear. It is likely that both national and global social and economic changes have produced conditions of increased stress in everyday life. Although there is little research that assesses the issue, it is also possible that there have been changes over the years in the capacity of children and adults to manage and cope with stressful situations and difficult emotions. Research clearly shows that children of permissive or indulgent parents have higher rates of behavioral and emotional problems than do children of authoritative parents. Child-centered parenting seeks to promote self-expression rather than behavioral inhibition in their children. These parents are also more reluctant to direct or set limits on children's emotional behavior. As a result, children of child-centered parents will likely have more difficulty developing effective strategies for emotional coping and behavioral regulation.

Other studies point to similar issues. For example, research suggests that there have been generational changes in what psychologists call "locus of control"—that is, one's sense of whether one's life is controlled by external forces or by one's own efforts.[5] Between 1960 and 2002, college students were increasingly likely to adopt an external locus of control, believing that their lives were more highly influenced by external circumstances than individual effort. This suggests that many young people feel that important aspects of their lives are largely beyond their control. This is to be expected if large numbers of recent generations of children have been the recipients of child-centered parenting. Children who feel entitled to

5. Lachman, M. E., Rosnick, C. B., & Röcke, C. (2009). The rise and fall of control beliefs and life satisfaction in adulthood: Trajectories of stability and change over ten years. In H. B. Bosworth, C. Hertzog (Eds.) , *Aging and cognition: Research methodologies and empirical advances* (pp. 143–160). Washington, DC, US: American Psychological Association.

Twenge, J. M., Zhang, L., & Im, C. (2004). It's beyond my control: A cross-temporal meta-analysis of increasing externality in locus of control, 1960–2002. *Personality and Social Psychology Review, 8*(3), 308–319.

have their needs met by others would be more likely to believe that good things would come easily. If I expect the world to come to me, I will be less likely to assume responsibility for my own fate. When the world fails to meet my expectations, I can claim clemency on the basis that the relevant circumstances were beyond my control.

The Good News: We Already Know How to Meet these Challenges

Parents who fear that the inculcation of moral values will rob children of the freedom to choose their own beliefs are likely to produce children who lack a moral compass. Children of parents who express their love by indulging their children's wishes tend to become narcissistic and self-focused. Parents who protect their children from experiencing negative emotions tend to produce children who are unable to cope with emotional stress. Adults who worry that too much direction or critical feedback will squash their child's creativity often fail to provide the very direction that a child needs to develop the creative skills the parent seeks to promote. Thus, while child-centered parenting has noble origins, it breeds a suite of unanticipated consequences.

How can parents be sensitive to a child's emotional well-being while at the same time promoting the emotional regulation, moral development, and a sense of purpose and achievement? Although these two sets of goals may seem to be opposing, in fact, they go together quite well.

The trick is to move beyond both child-centered and adult-centered ways of thinking about parenting. We need a view—one that brings together central insights of traditional (adult-centered) and progressive (child-centered) modes of parenting while discarding unwanted elements from both. Happily, we already know how to do this, and we've known it for a very long time. Decades of research and hundreds of studies clearly document the importance of both empathetic sensitivity and active guidance in fostering the development of responsible, emotionally secure, socially skilled children.

In the 1960s, Diana Baumrind identified three styles of parenting. *Authoritarian* parents maintain and enforce high maturity demands for their children, but are neither highly communicative nor empathetically nurturing with their children. In contrast, *permissive* parents are highly communicative and nurturing with their children, yet do not attempt to direct their children in terms of high maturity demands. (What I've called *child-centered parenting* shares much in common with permissive or indulgent parenting). *Authoritative* parents not only hold and enforce high maturity demands for the children, they are also highly nurturing and communicative. Children of authoritative parents proved to be vital, socially responsible, and more self-directed than children of either authoritarian or permissive parents.

Authoritative parents provide children with high levels of both structured direction and emotional support. There is no contradiction between these values. In fact, their combination is a tried-and-true formula for parenting success. In this way, authoritative parenting is old-school parenting. This book explains how to put authoritative parenting into action. In clear detail, it shows how to enjoy success as an old-school parent with modern-day kids.

KEY 1

VALUE YOUR
PARENTAL AUTHORITY

Authoritative parenting combines loving responsiveness with high-maturity demands.

==========

Old-school parenting is authoritative parenting. Authoritative parenting is not old school simply because it is "old fashioned." There are many things that are old fashioned that are best left in the past. Similarly, authoritative parenting is not old school simply because our grandparents may have used it. There are things that our grandparents did that we may not want to repeat. Instead, authoritative parenting is old school in the sense that it has stood the test of time. It worked back then; it works right now; and it will continue to work in the future. This is because authoritative parenting combines the two things that children need most: clear direction and responsive care.

Authoritative parents combine high expectations with loving nurturance. They are simultaneously demanding and responsive. They set high-maturity demands and help their children live up to those demands. They are fully aware that it is their job as parents to attempt to influence their children. However, they are also aware that children require loving guidance and understanding if they are to grow into responsible and competent adults.

Why have we tended to stray away from authoritative parenting? One answer lies in the way we think about the responsibilities we have toward our children. When we think of parenting, two ideas tend to come to mind: love and discipline. Parents love their children! We tend to feel that love is what fuels our desire to take care of and nurture our children. Because we love our kids, we would do anything for them. Parents also know that they have a responsibility to teach their children. They know they are responsible for teaching children right from wrong and proper from improper behavior.

Problems arise, however, when parents come to think that being loving is the opposite of promoting discipline. That is, a parent can either make her child feel loved or hold her child to high standards, but she cannot do both at the same time. To understand how authoritative parents produce competent children, it is first necessary to show that love and discipline are not opposite poles of a single dimension.

The Big Mistake: "Nice Parent, Mean Parent"

Figure 1.1 shows the big mistake that parents make in parenting. It occurs when we think of parenting as something that occurs along a single dimension or continuum. From this view, a parent is either strict or permissive, loving or demanding, nice or mean. Parents will often joke about being "nice" or "mean" to their children: "My son wanted to go to a friend's house before finishing his homework. I didn't let him, and he missed

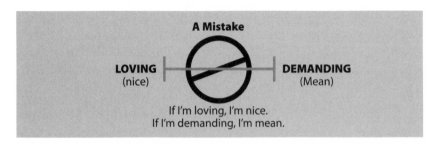

Figure 1.1. The Big Mistake

the chance to see his friend. I'm such a mean parent!" "She knows she can get whatever she wants from her Dad. He's the nice one. I'm the mean one." Although we tend to say these things in jest, jokes tend to have an element of truth in them. We often feel as if we are being mean to our children when we deny them what they want.

For example, at a birthday party for a relative, a parent wanted her four-year-old to say "thank you" after his grandmother gave him a gift. The child was unwilling to do so and was being quite defiant. Responding to her plea for help, I suggested that the mother require the child to sit in the corner until he was ready to say "thank you" to his grandmother. She agreed to try this. As she did, her face had an unintentional look of deep empathetic sadness. Her lips turned down into a sad, inverted U with her lower lip protruding out in a kind of pout. Her eyebrows were turned down in sadness and her forehead wrinkled. Her expression was deeply empathetic in the sense that she seemed to anticipate that her child would suffer from this intervention. She seemed to be sharing her son's suffering and didn't want to make him suffer! It is easy to believe that in this moment, the mother experienced herself as a "mean" parent.

Thinking of parenting in terms of "nice versus mean" is a trap. It gives us only two choices! Because we love our children, we want them to feel good. When we do something to make our children feel good, we are being nice. Because we have to teach children responsibility, we sometimes have to stop them from doing things that they want to do. This makes them feel bad.

For example, a two-and-a-half-year-old girl used paints to scribble a picture on the wall. Her mother, posting a photo of "Alison's artwork" on Facebook, complained, "and despite being watercolor, it is not washing off entirely." In response to a friend who posted "oops," the mother wrote, "No oops, it was fully intentional. She wanted to decorate the walls." This mother was struggling with the dilemma of whether to let her child use "harmless" watercolors to paint on the wall or restrict the girl's deliberate actions. To restrict the child's actions would make her feel badly. In the end, however, the mother who felt badly when she had difficulty cleaning up the child's mess. Acting out of love, Alison's mother was being "nice." As a result, however, Alison not only caused a mess for her mother but also failed to learn a lesson in self-control and the appropriate use of paints.

However, the mother could have easily acted out of love while simultaneously providing guidance and direction for her daughter. "Walls are not for painting. When you paint on the walls, it makes a mess that's hard to clean up! When we paint, we use an easel. Here! Paint me a beautiful picture on this easel." (It would also help if the mother placed the easel far away from a vacant wall so as not to distract the child.) In responding in this way, Alison's mother would have (1) encouraged Alison's interest (painting a picture) in a way that also (2) communicated a rule (we don't write on walls), (3) explained the reason for the rule (it makes a mess), and (4) provided an alternative way to meet Alison's interest (painting on the easel).

The trick to understanding authoritative parenting is to realize that being demanding (i.e., enforcing discipline, enforcing high standards, imposing maturity demands) and being responsive (i.e., attempting to encourage a child's interests, acknowledging a child's emotions, acting with loving care) are not opposite ends of a single dimension of parenting. Instead, they are two separate dimensions of parenting altogether. Parenting doesn't fall along a single "demanding ↔ responsive" dimension. Instead, demandingness and responsiveness are two separate dimensions. In any given situation, a parent can be more or less demanding ("more demanding ↔ less demanding") as well as more or less responsive ("more responsive ↔ less responsive"). Enforcing high standards is not the opposite of being loving and nurturing.

The Authoritative Parent: High Standards with Responsive Support

In groundbreaking work that she began in the 1960s and has continued to the present,[1] Diana Baumrind showed that there are systematic differences in the ways parents approach the task of parenting, and different parenting styles affect children in different ways. Since that time, research has identified at least four broad styles of parenting. Parents differ in two basic dimensions: the degree of demandingness and responsiveness.

Demandingness refers to the extent to which parents set and enforce high standards for their children's behavior. Parents who are demanding have high expectations for their children. They tend to use their differential power in an attempt to influence children and prompt them to live up to those expectations. Demanding parents tend to confront children's misbehavior directly; they tend to take a stand on children's behavior, even if doing so brings about parent–child conflict. They tend to monitor children's behavior in and out of the home and try to orient children toward parental values and desired outcomes throughout development. *Responsiveness* refers to the extent to which parents are sensitive to their children's emotional needs. Responsive parents are attuned to their children's needs and consider the needs, perspectives, and states of their children when interacting with them. Responsive parents are highly com-

1. Baumrind, D. (1966). Effects of authoritative parental control on child behavior. *Child Development*, 37(4), 887.

Baumrind, D. (1971). Current patterns of parental authority. *Developmental Psychology*, 4(1, Pt.2), 1–103.

Baumrind, D. (2005). Taking a stand in a morally pluralistic society: Constructive obedience and responsible dissent in moral/character education. In L. Nucci (Ed.) , *Conflict, contradiction, and contrarian elements in moral development and education* (pp. 21–50). Mahwah, NJ, US: Lawrence Erlbaum Associates Publishers.

Baumrind, D. (2012). Differentiating between confrontive and coercive kinds of parental power-assertive disciplinary practices. *Human Development*, 55(2), 35–51.

Baumrind, D. (2013). Authoritative parenting revisited: History and current status. In R. E. Larzelere, A. Morris, A. W. Harrist (Eds.) *Authoritative parenting: Synthesizing nurturance and discipline for optimal child development* (pp. 11–34). Washington, DC, US: American Psychological Association.

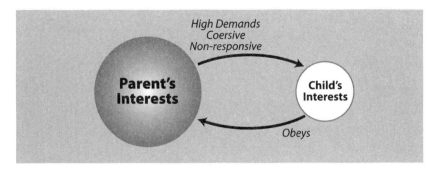

Figure 1.2. The Authoritarian Parenting Style

municative and interact with their children with warmth, love, nurturing, and acceptance. They tend to value reciprocity in parent–child interactions, show a willingness to adjust their behavior to the local wishes of children, and find ways to support children's attempts to influence their environments.

Authoritarian parents show high levels of demandingness and low levels of responsiveness. As shown in Figure 1.2, in an authoritarian parent–child relationship, the parent's interests dominate over the child's. Authoritarian parents have clear ideas of the types of standards to which they want their children to conform and of who they want their children to become. They tend to think of children in several related ways. First, authoritarian parents tend to believe that because they know more than their children, it is their job to socialize children in terms of the parent's beliefs and values. Because parents know more, they have authority over their children. Authoritarian parents value obedience; children are expected to respect parental authority and act accordingly. Second, authoritarian parents may think of children as if they were unformed lumps of clay that must be given shape. If children come into the world unshaped and unformed, it is the parent's job to shape a child's behavior so that it conforms to the parent's values and ideals. Finally, some authoritarian parents may think of children as inherently oppositional, with dispositions that are naturally contrary to a parent's authority. From this view, children are like wild horses and must be tamed or trained to follow the orders and directives of the parent. Because authoritarian parents value obedience to authority, they show low levels of responsiveness to children's needs; children are expected to conform to the wishes of parents, rather than vice versa.

Permissive or *indulgent* parents show a profile that is the direct opposite of that of authoritarian parents. Permissive parents show low levels of demandingness and high levels of responsiveness. Thus, in contrast to authoritarian parents, permissive parents allow their children's interests to dominant over their own. This is shown in Figure 1.3. Permissive parents tend to think of children in a series of different but related ways. Some permissive parents think of children as if they were budding flowers. From this romantic point of view, children are capable of directing their own development. They are born with a sense of inner direction that should be fostered and supported rather than thwarted. As budding flowers, children need warmth, sunshine, and fertile soil to grow. Too much direction from parents can halt development or cause children to develop along a false path. Other parents adopt a permissive style out of a desire to encourage independence, self-reliance, or initiative in their children. From this view, children can be taught to be self-reliant by providing them with the freedom to explore and control their worlds. Children learn through discovery, experimentation, and error. As a result, the most important thing that parents can do is provide their children with a loving,

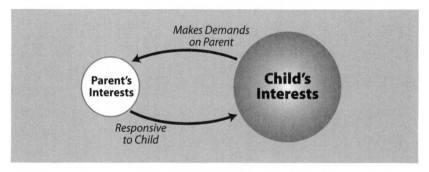

Figure 1.3. The Permissive Parenting Style

warm, and emotionally safe environment in which to develop and grow.

Authoritative parents exhibit both high levels of demandingness and high levels of responsiveness. Authoritative parents recognize that their children are separate individuals with their own developing interests. However, they also believe that their children are incomplete beings who require guidance to develop into full-fledged persons who are capable of living successfully in society. Thus, as shown in Figure 1.4, while maintaining their authority, authoritative parents attempt to coordinate their own interests, standards, and rules with the legitimate interests, needs, and perspectives of their children. Like authoritarian parents, authoritative parents take a firm stance on their children's behavior and attempt to bring that behavior in line with their beliefs and values. However, unlike authoritarian parents, authoritative parents are not coercive. They refrain from using threats, empty promises, and punishments as vehicles to influence their children. Instead, against the backdrop of clear limits and high expectations, they use reasoning to explain the basis of family rules and show the importance of those rules for the developing child.

Like permissive parents, authoritative parents are sensitive to their children's emotional needs and wishes. They are highly communicative, accepting, and responsive to their children's needs. However, unlike permissive parents, authoritative parents do not relinquish their authority when interacting with children. They seek to establish authentic communication with

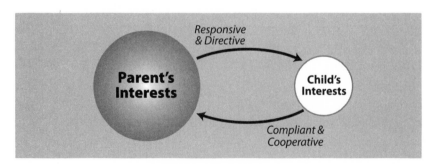

Figure 1.4. The Authoritative Parenting Style

their children. That is, they are clear and honest in communicating their expectations and needs. Whenever possible, authoritative parents attempt to advance their children's interests and desires—within the parameters set by the parent's values and expectations. Thus, although authoritative parents are sensitive to their children's wishes, they do not allow children to make choices that fall outside of the parent's limits and expectations. In this way, authoritative parents promote children's autonomy not by leaving them to their own devices, but by equipping them with the skills, knowledge, and emotional resources they need to make effective choices as they approach adulthood.

Disengaged parents exhibit low levels of both demandingness and responsiveness. These parents tend to be uninvolved in their children's lives and indifferent to them, and they place self-concerns above those of their children. Parents who are disengaged may be emotionally distant, may be insensitive, or simply fail to interact with their children. Alternatively, disengaged parents may be actively dismissing of their children's emotional needs. This style of parenting occurs in a variety of different homes. These can include high-income homes where parents are more focused on careers than on their children, low-income families where parents work multiple jobs to make ends meet, or families that exhibit high levels of dysfunctionality. Regardless of the source, disengaged parents fail to provide the degree of love, acceptance, and security that responsive parents provide or the level of control, regulation, and maturity expectations that demanding parents do. As a result, the intellectual, social, and emotional outcomes of children of disengaged parents tend to be quite poor.

How Different Parenting Styles Affect Children's Development

In her original research program, Baumrind studied the relationship between different parenting styles and the development of what she called instrumental competence in children. *Instrumental competence* refers to the extent to which children are generally competent in four basic modes of behaving: social responsibility, independence, achievement orientation, and vitality. Socially responsible children are able to get along well with peers and adults. They are friendly with others, cooperative, and supportive rather than disruptive of the work of peers. Independent children are able to direct their own age-appropriate activities without constant direction and intervention from adults. They are able to be assertive and purposeful while at the same time being sensitive to the needs of others. Achievement-oriented children are those who seek or accept intellectual challenge both in and out of school. They are able to solve problems effectively and persistently without being impulsive and overly dependent on others. Finally, vitality simply refers to a child's everyday level of biological energy and well-being. Children who show vitality are those who approach everyday life with enthusiasm and vigor rather than apathy or disinterest.

Baumrind found that children of authoritative parents tended to show higher levels of instrumental competence than did children of either authoritarian or permissive parents. (Baumrind did not study disengaged parents in her original groundbreaking research.) Children of authoritative parents tended to be assertive and purposeful, cooperative and friendly, active and energetic while also showing strong motivation toward achievement. In contrast, children of authoritarian parents tended to be more withdrawn, showing less energy and vitality in everyday tasks. They tended to be shyer and more withdrawn around their peers. Children of permissive parenting showed many of the same behaviors. They showed lower levels of independence, self-control, and vitality than did children of authoritative parents.

Why do children of authoritative parents turn out be the most instrumentally competent? The reason is that authoritative parents provide children with both clear direction and responsive support. High standards and maturity demands are necessary to provide the direction for children's development. High levels of responsive nurturance are necessary to provide the emotional support that children need to confront the changing challenges and demands of life. Think of all of the learning a child has to do over the course of development. Imagine that a child had to confront all that learning alone. How could she do it? Without guidance, she would not know what to do. Without emotional support, she would feel overwhelmed by the challenges of everyday life. Children need both guidance and support. That is what authoritative parents provide.

It may seem surprising that children of authoritarian and permissive parents tend to show similar profiles of behavior — namely, relatively low levels of instrumental competence. After all, authoritarian and permissive parents treat their children in largely opposite ways. Why do their children turn out similarly? As just stated, children need both clear direction and responsive support. Authoritarian parents provide direction without the responsive support; permissive parents provide support without direction. As a result, children of permissive parents come to feel loved, but fail to develop an inner sense of direction. Children of authoritarian parents know what is expected of them, but often fail to develop the inner security and self-assuredness necessary to direct their own lives and maintain mutually supportive relationships with others.

Raising children is largely about teaching them how to adapt to the demands of everyday life. Human children require 20 years (or more) to reach adulthood. No other species spends so much time developing outside of the mother's womb; no other animal requires that much time to reach maturity. Why is this? As adults, humans are the most complex and sophisticated animals ever to walk the Earth. Relative to who they will become as adults, human infants are vastly incomplete beings. They need those 20 (plus) years to actualize their developmental potential. In other words, they need two decades of interaction with their environments to become fully developed.

Children can't do it on their own. They need the love and guidance of parents (and other socialization agents) to complete them.

What Do Authoritarian, Permissive, and Authoritative Parenting Styles Look Like?

What do different parenting styles look like? Let's examine how authoritarian, permissive, and authoritative parents tend to interact with children in three different disciplinary situations. First, it is important to understand that authoritarian, permissive, and authoritative parenting are different *styles* of parenting. They are more or less general ways in which parents approach the task of childrearing. For a pattern of parenting behavior to be considered a style, it has to be something that tends to happen relatively frequently over time. As parents, we are never entirely consistent in our behavior. Few parents are authoritarian, permissive, or authoritative all the time. On occasion, virtually all parents will find themselves using power assertion to enforce compliance in their children, "giving in" to a child's whining and complaining, or even being emotionally unavailable to a child. Even though individual parents never act in any one way all the time, general styles of parenting do exist. Let's take a look at some of the ways authoritarian, permissive, and authoritative parents tend to respond to children.

At the Market

The scene is the grocery market. The parent is checking out with a five-year-old child in tow. The child eyes some candy as the parent interacts with the clerk. The child asks for some candy.

A Permissive Solution: Giving In

Five-year-old Mattie asks her mother to buy her some candy. Her mother denies her request, saying, "No sweets until after you eat your dinner." At this point, Mattie begins to beg her mother for candy. The mother first replies by saying "No." As Mattie continues to whine, her mother explains her position further by saying, "No candy before dinner," and "You have to wait until after dinner." Soon, Mattie's mom becomes more frustrated: "You can't have something every time you go to the store!" Over time, Mattie's voice becomes more and more whiny and annoying. She is in danger of causing a scene. Frustrated and embarrassed, her mother says, "Oh, all right," and buys the candy. Mattie is silent, and Mom is relieved.

Mom may be relieved for now, but her solution to the problem is not permanent. In this situation, she makes the mistake of continuing to negotiate with Mattie and tolerate her whining after having already said "no." By continuing to respond to Mattie's pleas, her mother essentially defines the situation as a kind of open negotiation. The girl is able to think something akin to, "If Mom is open to my questions, then maybe I can convince her!" As a result, she learns that her incessant whining is effective in keeping Mom engaged. When her finally mother gives in, Mattie learns that she can use the strategy of incessant whining to get what she wants. Conversely, her mother has learned that she can get Mattie to stop whining by giving her what she wants.

In this context, the mother's behavior is permissive because she fails to enforce clear and firm limits on Mattie's behavior. She responds to Mattie's repeated requests by honoring them, even though she did not want to do so. The mother may feel that she is being responsive to Mattie; after all, she is making her happy by giving her something that she wants. However, Mattie's mother is not so much being responsive as she is being manipulated. Because Mattie's mother fails to enforce clear limits, Mattie is essentially able to hold her mother hostage: either you buy me some candy, or I'll keep whining. As a result, Mattie learns to assert her interests without learning the need to respect the interests of her mother.

An Authoritarian Solution: Coercive Power Assertion

Zack and his mother are in the check-out aisle. After Zack makes a request, his mother replies with a stern "No." Zack is silent. After a minute or so, he asks again. At this point, his mother says, "You heard what I said! I already said 'no.' Now it's no dessert at all after dinner." Zack begins to cry.

In this situation, Mom has effectively stopped Zack from begging for candy. She has won in a battle of the wills with her son. However, she has won only because she has superior power. This solution to the problem brings a series of negative outcomes. First, it does not help Zack learn anything about the basis of Mom's rule—something like, "If you eat candy now, you won't want to eat your dinner." More important, it fails to teach Zack more effective ways of getting what he wants (e.g., by asking politely and delaying gratification until later). Most important, it does nothing to promote a secure partnership between Zack and his mother. Zack learns that if he wants something sweet, he'll have to go around his mother and steal a cookie to get it. In this situation, the mother's behavior is authoritarian because she forces her child into compliance by using her superior power and fails to respond in ways that are sensitive to Zack's emotional needs—particularly, his need to feel heard and appreciated by his mother.

An Authoritative Strategy: Responsive Limit Setting

Pat and her mother are almost ready to leave the store. Pat begins to beg her mother for candy. As she does, her mother responds by saying, "I know that you want some candy. However I don't want you to have candy before dinner. Last time, when you ate candy before dinner, you didn't finish your meal. Now, stop asking for candy right now. If you continue to whine, I am not going to respond to you."

Pat's mother responds to her whining by being both responsive and directive. She is responsive by acknowledging Pat's feelings and request ("I know that you want some candy") and explaining why she doesn't want Pat to have candy before dinner. However, the mother is directive by establishing clear limits (i.e., no more whining) and by identifying the types of meaningful consequences that will occur should Pat continue her whining ("I am not going to respond to you."). If Pat's mother has been consistent in setting clear boundaries in the past, it is likely that Pat will know that her mother means what she says.

If Pat continues to whine and ask for candy, it is important that her mother follow through on her promise to not respond. In so doing, Pat would find that her requests fail to work as she intended. When a child's actions fail to yield the intended consequences, he or she is usually motivated to change her behavior. In this situation, after a few rounds of asking, Pat would be likely to give up. If she did not, her mother—with or without warning—might choose simply to take her out of the store. Such an action would communicate clearly to Pat that she is unable to advance her interests (getting candy) by continuing to whine.

In addition to setting clear and firm limits, it would also be helpful for Pat's mother to teach Pat an alternative way she can advance her interests. The mother might say, for example: "I know that you want some candy. However, whining and asking over and over again is not the way to get what you want. If you want some candy, you can ask me politely if I could buy you something for after dinner. You can say, 'Mom, can you buy me a Snickers bar for after dinner?' You can either do that or sit quietly here until I'm done checking out the groceries."

Such an action shows the child that the parent cares about what the child wants. Simply stopping a child from engaging in some unwanted behavior is not enough to bring about long-term changes in behavior. By showing Pat an alternative way to advance her interests, her mom is showing her how to do so appropriately. This interaction is authoritative because the mother is both responsive to Pat's interests and needs while also providing alternative and appropriate ways to advance those interests.

Facing a Challenge

A nine-year-old child is working on math homework. The child is learning multiplication tables but is having difficulty. She knows the five tables, but is having trouble with the six tables. The child and parent are using flash cards. The parent begins to show the child the flashcards: "What is six times one?" The child begins to have trouble with "What is six times two?"

A Permissive Response: Letting the Child Lead

MOM: What's six times two?

MATTIE: I don't know.

MOM: Well, try. How would you figure it out?

MATTIE: Count on my fingers?

MOM: Sure—go ahead.

MATTIE: 1-2-3-4-5-6 . . . but now what do I do?

MOM: What do you think?

MATTIE: This is stupid. Why do I have to do this? Can we be finished now?

MOM: You are going to need to know math when you are a grown-up.

MATTIE: I don't want to do this.

MOM: Okay, take a break. We'll start again later.

In this situation, when Mattie begins to have trouble with her six tables, her mother begins by asking, "How would you figure it out?" This is a good question. When teaching children, you can get an idea of what the child understands before trying to teach the next step. Asking an open-ended question like "How would you do it?" encourages the child to use her present knowledge to try to solve a problem. Mattie suggested a good strategy—counting on her fingers. When that strategy failed, she asked her mother for help. At this point, wanting Mattie to continue to try to figure out the solution for herself—and perhaps not sensing her growing frustration—her mother again asked her to try for herself. As Mattie's frustration grew, she began to seek a way out of the task. Her mother tried to convince her to continue by explaining that math would be important. Unconvinced, Mattie continued to protest, complaining that the task was too difficult. Sensing Mattie's frustration, and not wanting to tax her further, her mother suggested a break.

Mattie's mother engaged in the permissive strategy of allowing the child to lead the learning activity. Following the child's lead is a preferred strategy among many child-centered parents. This is based on the well-intentioned idea that children learn best through the process of active discovery. From this perspective, although children may learn from direct instruction, such instruction is more likely to produce rote memorization rather than deep understanding. Deep and lasting learning is thought to be that which is self-directed and under the child's control.

This well-intentioned idea only addresses half of the process of teaching and learning. It is true that the best learning occurs when children are intellectually and emotionally engaged with their learning. However, this does not mean that children are able to create all new knowledge on their own. The interaction with Mattie started well—she suggested a useful strategy for multiplying six times two. When that strategy failed, Mattie needed additional support and direction to figure out how to make it work. When her mother turned the task back over to Mattie, the girl became frustrated and wanted to stop. At that point, Mattie was in need of two types of assistance: help in solving the math problem and help in managing her emotions in a way that would allow her to persevere and achieve success.

Because the mother was committed to letting Mattie set the terms of the interaction, she deferred to Mattie's protests, choosing to let her daughter take a break rather than helping her find ways to manage her frustration in ways that would support her learning.

An Authoritarian Strategy: Unilateral Control

DAD: What's six times two?

ZACK: I don't know."

DAD: Well, try. How did your teacher tell you to figure it out?

ZACK: Count on my fingers?

DAD: Your teacher didn't tell you to count on your fingers. Only little kids count on fingers. We have to memorize the six tables. What's six times one?

ZACK: Six

DAD: Good. What's six times two?

ZACK: (*Starting to count on his fingers*)

DAD: No—we don't count. Six times two is 12. Say 'Six times two is twelve."

ZACK: Six times two is 12.

DAD: Now, six times three is 18 . . .

In this situation, the parent adopts the opposite strategy of the permissive parent. To be sure, in this situation, Zack's father has high-maturity demands. He wants his child to learn the multiplication tables. He also has clear ideas about *how* Zack should learn his multiplication tables—he wants him to commit math facts to memory. Learning math facts is an important part of learning multiplication.[2] However, while Zack's father

---

2. Learning math facts—committing addition and multiplication tables to memory—is a useful and important skill that parents and educators should promote in children. However, it is only one part of what a child needs to learn to understand multiplication. A full understanding of multiplication also requires that children acquire an understanding of (1) the

has high-maturity demands, he is neither sensitive to the nature of Zack's difficulty nor responsive to his son's emotional state. When Zack experienced difficulty, the father simply took over the task, essentially forcing the boy to learn using the strategy the father felt was best. As a result, the father both rejected and derogated Zack's own attempts to solve the problem (counting on his fingers). The father's coercive strategy not only failed to help Zack regulate the frustration and distress that accompanied the task, it exacerbated the negative emotion produced in this situation.

An Authoritative Solution: Supportive Direction

Mom: What's six times two?

Pat: I don't know.

Mom: Well, let's try. How would you figure it out?

Pat: Count on my fingers?

Mom: Sure—go ahead.

Pat: 1-2-3-4-5-6 . . . (*holding up six fingers*) But now what do I do? I only have four fingers left!

Mom: I see. You have four fingers left! What can you do?

Pat: I can count up four more.

Mom: Go ahead. Give it a try.

Pat: 7-8-9-10 . . . but that's still only four more. We need six more. Let's start again.

Mom: Hold on—let's keep trying this. If it doesn't work, we'll start again. There are a lot of different ways to multiply six times two.

Pat: Okay. What do I do?

---

concept of multiplication itself; (2) multiple ways to calculate different types of multiplication problems; (3) how multiplication is related to addition and division; (4) how to apply multiplicative knowledge to different types of word problems; and so forth. Children who learn math facts often have an advantage in acquiring such higher order skills than children who have not.

Mom: You added four more, right? How many more than four is six?

Pat: Two!

Mom: You are holding up 10 fingers. Add two to that and what do you get?

Pat: Twelve. Six plus six is 12.

The mother's authoritative approach differs substantially from the permissive and authoritarian responses. Pat's mother was simultaneously responsive and directive throughout the teaching and learning experience. Similar to the permissive approach (Mattie's mother), Pat's mother began their interaction by asking Pat how she might solve the problem. Like the permissive approach, Pat's mother encouraged her to use her selected strategy. This is in contrast to the authoritarian approach, in which Zack's father discouraged him from trying his own strategy. Once Pat's strategy failed, however, her mother provided additional support and direction to help Pat figure out how to perform the problem. As the problem became more difficult, Pat sought ways to simplify the problem (wanting to start over). Her mother, sensing that Pat might be successful if she continued, provided additional support and direction. As a result, Pat not only solved the problem in an unusual and clever way, she was also able to tolerate the emotional aspects of working through the problem. Over time, such interactions foster the development of intellectual (i.e., deep learning), social (i.e., interaction with her mother), and emotional skills (i.e., managing emotion).

Managing Mischief

Although it is increasingly uncommon, there are occasions in which adults other than a child's parents play a role in regulating a child's behavior. Here is a description of a situation involving a seven-year-old boy, his permissive mother, and an authoritative adult during a church party. In separate interactions involving his mother and other children, the boy engaged in a series of intrusive acts (i.e., pulling his mother's necklace off of her neck, scaring a boy, teasing another boy). The boy, undeterred by his mother's placid prohibitions, continued his misbehavior unabated. However, he proved able to rein in his behavior when disciplined in an authoritative manner by another adult.

Mavis and her son, seven-year-old Derrick, were attending a party at church. Mavis was having a conversation with adults April and Bob. Derrick was playing with other children. Mavis was wearing long, beautiful stretch necklace. Derrick wanted the necklace. He jumped up, put his hands on the necklace, and pulled it. Mavis adjusted her posture—leaned her head to the side—both so that her necklace could come off easily and to avoid the possibility of injury. Derrick pulled the necklace off his mother, disheveling her hair. Adjusting her hair, Mavis said quietly, "Oh Derrick, don't do that," and continued with the conversation.

As the children continued playing, one boy ran past Derrick with a drink. Derrick jumped front of the boy and yelled, "Rahhh!" The other boy drew back, managing not to spill his drink. With a frown, the child moved on. Mavis turned toward Derrick and said, "Don't do that." Derrick simply laughed. At this point, April chimed in: "Derrick, when you do something like that, it's unexpected. You could have spilled his drink and it could have made a mess. He is not gonna feel real good about that, right?" Looking thoughtful and serious, Derrick nodded his head and said, "right," indicating his understanding of what April was saying. Mavis watched the interaction quietly without acknowledgment. April returned to her conversation with Mavis and Bob.

Soon thereafter, Derrick began to tease another child in close proximity to the adults. April turned and made eye contact with Derrick; her look was friendly, but serious. Derrick immediately hesitated and stopped what he was doing.

In this situation, it is possible to argue that the seven-year-old boy was merely engaged in some harmless horseplay. From this view, there is nothing terribly unusual about the boy's behavior. When playing together, kids this age tease each other playfully, play jokes on each other, and engage in all forms of harmless mischief. Although it may have been bad form for the boy to pull the necklace from his mother's neck, no real harm was done—especially if the mother didn't really mind the action. Why shouldn't a child be able to play with his mother's necklace? What makes that such a bad thing?

This is deeply permissive thinking. To be sure, all parents want the best for their children. Many parents, however, take this sentiment to mean that being a loving parent means doing what they can to make their child happy. From here, it is only a short step to the mistaken idea that being a loving parent means making children experience good feelings while protecting them from bad ones. This sort of reasoning puts parents in a bind. Placing maturity demands on a child necessarily limits that child's freedom and spontaneity. If granting children broad freedoms allows them to feel good, then restricting those freedoms will make them feel bad. A parent who believes that being loving means fostering good feelings is likely to find it difficult to discipline a child. It is as if the parent reasons like this: "Loving parents do not cause pain; discipline causes pain; loving parents do not discipline."

It is likely that Mavis found it difficult to place limits over Derrick's behavior because she felt that doing so would deprive him of happiness. It is also clear that she did not entirely approve of her son's behavior; she did, after all, make attempts to discourage his behavior, even if those attempts were weak and ineffective. The fact that another adult was able to influence the boy's behavior by putting forth clearly defined limits suggests that the boy's incapacity to regulate his behavior is something that can be altered by establishing an authoritative parent–child relationship.

If Mavis continues her permissive style of parenting Derrick, she will be trading his short-term pleasure for his long-term well-being. Loving parents want the best for their children. However, loving parents also know that children are not necessarily in the position to know what is best for them. That's what parents are for.

Task 1.1. What Is Your Parenting Profile?

1. Your child likes to eat noodles and tomato sauce. Tonight you are having baked fish, potatoes, and broccoli. Your child refuses to eat. You:
   a. make him noodles and sauce.
   b. tell your child that he can either eat or not eat the family meal, and that it is too much to expect you to make something special for him.
   c. tell your child that he can make himself a peanut butter and jelly sandwich (or something similar), but that he must try each of the foods first.

2. Your child is afraid of a new cat that approaches her. You:
   a. pick up the cat and take it away.
   b. put yourself between your child and the cat and encourage her to pet the cat.
   c. do nothing and allow your child to learn how to approach the cat on her own.

3. Helping children with their homework:
   a. Robs them of the opportunity to learn by doing it for themselves.
   b. is important to help children learn.
   c. gives children an excuse not to do it themselves.
   d. should only occur when children don't know how to do the work themselves.

4. Your teen speaks disrespectfully to you. You:
   a. punish him by grounding him for a week.
   b. inform him that you will not respond to him until he speaks to you in a respectful way.
   c. explain that you feel hurt when he talks to you that way.

5. Which best describes your approach to raising children?
   a. Children need guidance and direction. If a child does something wrong, they should be punished.
   b. The most important thing to do is to give children love and affection; they will eventually learn to follow their own path.
   c. Parents have to set clear rules but also be open to a child's perspective.

6. When you think about child rearing, which of the following values is most important to you?
   a. Compliance
   b. Cooperation
   c. Self-esteem

7. Your child grabs a toy from a friend. You:
   a. punish your child (e.g., take away his toys, send him to his room)
   b. say, "how would you like it if someone grabbed a toy from you?" Tell the child to apologize and return the toy.
   c. encourage the children to work out the conflict for themselves.

8. From your perspective, a child is:
   a. like a budding flower—if a child has sunshine, water, and good soil, he or she will blossom.
   b. an incomplete person who needs guidance and sensitivity to develop.
   c. like a stallion—a child has a will of his own that often has to be broken to develop into a civilized person.
   d. like clay—a child has his own dispositions, but it is the parent's job to try to mold or shape the child to become a good person or citizen.

9. Your child shares his candy with a friend without being asked. You:
   a. tell her, "It's good of you to think of your friend!"
   b. say, "Great job! You're such a good girl!"
   c. say nothing, as a child should not have to be rewarded for doing the right thing.

10. Your preteen has not been doing his chores. He has been playing video games instead. You:
    a. punish him (e.g., take away privileges, ground him).
    b. set up a time for your child to do chores as you monitor him.
    c. cut down on his chores to make them more manageable.

11. When my child does something wrong:
    a. I ask him not to do it again.
    b. I make sure he gets some sort of punishment.
    c. I explain what my child did wrong.

12. When my child is upset, I tend to:
    a. calm her by removing her from the upsetting situation.
    b. show her how to fix the upsetting situation.
    c. expect her to be "suck it up" or "tough it out" for herself.

13. Which of the following statements do you most agree with?
    a. Explaining what a child did wrong tends to be a waste of time; children need consequences, not explanations.
    b. Explanations give children reasons to act properly.
    c. Children need to learn to find their own reasons for why something is right or wrong.

14. Your child throws a tantrum in public. You:
    a. calm him down by buying him an ice cream cone or something similar.
    b. tell him to stop crying or he will be punished.
    c. take him out of the store and let him finish his tantrum without responding to him.

15. Which of the following statements do you most agree with?
    a. It is important for a child to have self-esteem before he or she can be successful at something.
    b. Self-esteem must be earned by learning to do things well.
    c. Self-esteem is mostly irrelevant; children need to learn to live up to their parents' and teachers' expectations regardless of how they feel about themselves.

Answer Key

	Tend Toward Authoritarian	Tend Toward Permissive	Tend Toward Authoritative
1	b	a	c
2	c	a	b
3	c	a	b or d
4	a	c	b
5	a	b	c
6	a	c	b
7	a	c	b
8	c or d	a	b
9	c	b	a
10	a	c	b
11	b	a	c
12	c	a	b
13	a	c	b
14	b	a	c
15	c	a	a
Total Answers			

Task 1.2. Your Parents' Parenting

How were you raised? What was your parents' parenting style? How are you different from your parents? Take this quiz to find out. Because parents often differ in their parenting styles, you might choose to take the quiz several times—once for each caregiver in your child's life. To complete the quiz, simply check "yes" or "no" for each question. When you have finished, use the key provided and add up your parents' authoritarian, permissive, and authoritative scores. Parents often show a mixture of parenting styles.

As I Was Growing Up, My Parent . . .	Yes	No
1 believed that I should be given as much freedom as possible.		
2 often forced me to follow rules that I didn't agree with.		
3 expected me to follow directives immediately without asking questions.		
4 discussed the reasoning behind family rules.		
5 encouraged me to discuss family rules that I felt were unreasonable.		
6 felt that I should be free to make my own decisions even if they disagreed.		
7 made expectations clear, but allowed me to discuss those expectations if I thought they were unreasonable.		
8 felt that I should know who the boss was in the family.		
9 seldom set guidelines for my behavior.		
10 tended to do what the children wanted when making family decisions.		
11 guided and directed me but also provided a rationale for why I should do what was suggested.		
12 would become upset if I tried to disagree with him or her.		
13 believed that children suffer from parents who put too many restrictions on them.		
14 let me know what was expected of me and punished me if I didn't meet expectations.		
15 allowed me to decide most things for myself without interfering.		

16 took my opinions into consideration when making family decisions, but did not decide something simply because I wanted it.

17 did not view him- or herself as responsible for directing or guiding my behavior.

18 had clear standards for behavior, but was willing to adjust them if I raised good reasons why they should be changed.

19 directed my behavior and activities but was willing to listen to my concerns and discuss them with me.

20 allowed me to form my own point of view on family matters and generally allowed me to decide for myself what I was going to do.

21 was strict with me.

22 expected me to do things exactly as he or she said it should be done.

23 gave me clear guidance and direction, but was also understanding when I disagreed.

24 insisted that I conform to his or her expectations simply out of respect for his or her authority.

Answer Key

To calculate your scores for each mode of parenting, go through each column and put a check next to each question that you said "yes". Then add up the number of questions ("yes's") you checked for each mode of parenting. Your score on each parenting mode is the number of questions you've checked. Some parents find that parenting mode is more dominant for them than others (that is, that they tend to use mainly an authoritative, permissive or authoritarian mode); other parents find they use more than one parenting mode. Don't be surprised if you find that you use of mixture of different approaches in different situations!

	Authoritarian Questions	Which Did You Check "Yes"?	Permissive Questions	Which Did You Check "Yes"?	Authoritative Questions	Which Did You Check "Yes"?
1	2		1		4	
2	3		6		5	
3	8		9		7	
4	12		10		11	
5	14		13		16	
6	21		15		18	
7	22		17		19	
8	24		20		23	
	Authoritarian Score		**Permissive Score**		**Authoritative Score**	

KEY 2

CULTIVATE YOUR
CHILD'S CHARACTER

The key to raising competent, responsible, and socially sensitive children is to foster the development of moral self-cultivation.

In the movie *Murphy's Romance*, Murphy Jones (James Garner), becomes romantically interested in Emma Moriarty (Sally Field), a divorced mother with a 12-year-old son named Jake. Bobby Jack, Emma's ne're-do-well ex-husband, arrives on the scene, trying to woo Emma back. At one point in the movie, Emma, Murphy, Bobby, and Jake are enjoying a game of cards at Emma's ranch house. Bobby Jack begins to cheat. Murphy notices and, calling Bobby Jack outside for a private chat, calls him on his cheating.

Later on, there is a scene in which Murphy and Jake share a moment on a bench in the middle of town. The following dialogue occurs:

JAKE (*earnestly*): I saw what my dad did when we were playing cards.

MURPHY (*after a pause*): Maybe it's a good thing you did.

JAKE: He did it twice.

MURPHY: Take after him or not, it's up to you.

Murphy communicates a great deal of meaning in this simple statement: "Take after him or not, it's up to you." This phrase communicates two basic points. First, Murphy seems to be saying, "Your future is up to you. I can't choose for you—you've got to choose for yourself." The second and more important meaning is communicated by the phrase "take after him or not." With these few words, Murphy holding up a set of images for the boy. He holds up two pictures of the kind of person Jake can become. In this case, Murphy is saying the boy can be dishonest or honest. He can be a cheat, or he can be a good sport.

Murphy is concerned about Jake's character—the type of person that Jake can become. What is character? A person's *character* is not the same as an individual's personality. By personality, we mean an individual's general pattern of thinking, feeling, and action—whether the person is outgoing or inhibited, calm or excitable, open or closed to new experiences, and so on.

Character, however, has a moral component. It refers to a person's moral orientation. To speak of a person's character is to speak of his or her capacity to bring his or her behavior in line with moral ideals. It refers to the goodness of a person—an individual's capacity to act as a moral or virtuous person.

The Meaning and Value of Moral Character

Moral character refers to the more or less consistent disposition to act in accordance with a system of moral values. The concept of moral character is an old one. In Western culture, we can trace it at least as far back as Aristotle. For Aristotle, to have moral character is to achieve moral goodness. We develop moral character by cultivating virtue. Virtues are moral qualities (e.g., courage, compassion, gratitude, trustworthiness, effort). We are not born with moral character; it is something we must cultivate slowly over time. For Aristotle, the path to moral character is clear and direct: to cultivate virtue, we must act in virtuous ways. Over time, the more we practice virtue, the more it becomes part of who we are. Kind habits develop by repeating kind actions; we cultivate a compassionate disposition by repeatedly performing compassionate acts.

Moral character is not easy to cultivate. It is not something a child can acquire simply by himself. In child development, the acquisition of complex skills tends to move from other-regulation to self-regulation. Children first develop new skills in interactions with other people (e.g., parents, teachers, other children) and only later gain some degree of mastery of those new skills. For example, children do not learn to tell time spontaneously on their own. They develop the skill first under tutelage of adults, only later becoming able to tell the time by themselves. This is true for the development of virtue as well. A parent might say, "It is important to be helpful when we are clearing the table. Here—take this dish into the kitchen." This is not to say, of course, that young children are not already disposed to respond in helpful, caring and morally sensitive ways. They are. It is only to say that such dispositions develop under the sensitive guidance and support of other people.

To cultivate moral character is to attempt to act in accordance with a particular image of oneself. It requires the active attempt to become a certain type of person—a person who displays qualities of moral goodness (virtue). It is a form of self-cultivation. There are two senses in which this is the case. First, cultivating moral character involves cultivating the self—cultivating one's sense of what it means to be a good person, and then acting in accordance with that image. Second, the task of self-cultivation is something that is ultimately accomplished *by* the self, although with the guidance and support of a sensitive and responsible adult. As a result, the job of the parent becomes one of helping the child construct, appreciate, and identify a sense of what it means to be a good person, showing children how to act in accordance with that image, and making children accountable for doing so.

Some people might think of the process of self-cultivation as arduous—requiring constant self-sacrifice or the need to control one's desires. The process of self-cultivation is actually quite common. Older children's participation in sports and other physical activities provides a particularly good example of the process of self-cultivation. Teens who become involved in sports tend to become highly invested in developing a certain type of valued identity. They want to both see themselves and be seen as good football players, dancers, or gymnasts. These children are willing to endure considerable discomfort to build the skills (and shape their bodies) to achieve such valued identities.

Self-cultivation in the moral arena is similar to the process of self-cultivation in sports. Both involve movement toward a valued goal or end (e.g., becoming a good football player, becoming a good person), receiving instruction, and engaging in effortful action intended to move toward the goal. The two processes differ, however, in the extent to which they are generally valued in our culture. At this moment, there is arguably more consensus about the meaning and value of being a good athlete than there is about being a good person. (This is not a ubiquitous condition across the world's cultures. Sports are not as popular a cultural institution, for example, in China.)

To foster the development of moral character, the parent's job becomes one of helping the child identify with and act on a system of moral values. In a pluralistic culture such as our own, this is not always an easy thing to do; children socialized into one set of values may find that others do not share those values. This is no reason to abandon the goal of character development. It simply means that there is a need to teach children to engage constructively with those who hold different value systems. Engaging others constructively does not mean simply accommodating to values of the other. It means genuinely engaging in an exploration of the meaning of difference. On some occasions, our engagements may motivate us to modify our selves in the direction of the other; on other occasions, the opposite may occur. In still other circumstances, partners may accommodate to each other or remain unchanged. Regardless of the outcome, we cultivate our selves through our relationships with others. Thus, engaging diverse value systems is not the enemy of self-cultivation; on the contrary, it is part of its very process.

Thus, the process of moral self-cultivation is both open-ended and constrained. It is constrained by the virtues and values a parent seeks to cultivate in his or her child. It is open-ended in the sense that as he develops the capacity for self-reflection in social interactions, the child himself will assume the primary role of identifying the values that will define his moral identity. As this occurs over time, the child's motives and way of being in the world become transformed. Having developed an inner compass, the child will be increasingly able to direct his own actions in term of his values and personal goals. Let's explore how this happens.

Fostering Moral Self-Cultivation in Children

The key to fostering character development is to direct children through the noble craft of moral self-cultivation. Self-cultivation is the active attempt to improve oneself gradually over time. It is the long-term commitment to becoming a certain type of person over time. It reflects the lifelong endeavor to fashion oneself according to one's (constantly evolving) image of who one should be as a person. From this view, it is the job of parents to actively direct, guide, or otherwise assist children to identify with and act on some system of moral values and is to draw on a child's already existing desire to be seen as good by both himself and others. The parents' job is to show children how to behave so that they can be seen by themselves and others as good persons. It is as if the parent says, "A good person is someone who is responsible, caring, honest, and so on. These qualities are important because of A, B, and C. It's your job to try to become a responsible, caring, honest person; it's my job to help you get there."

This is old-school parenting—and it may rub against the grain of some modern sensibilities, particularly the tendency of child-centered parents to yield authority to children in the name of granting them autonomy. It is not possible to cultivate character in children without taking a stand on the types of moral qualities one wishes to promote in them. Children are incomplete beings; they require at least two decades of parenting to develop into competent and responsible adults. As they grow older, they will have more of a say in determining the types of people that they wish to become. Until that time arrives, they need moral guidance from trusted people who know better than they do. Those people are the child's parents.

Fostering the Self-Cultivation Mindset

The task of fostering long-term self-cultivation in children requires a significant shift away from child-centered thinking. It requires that parents direct our children's attention not simply to who they are right now but also to the type of person we want them to become in the future. However, many contemporary parents have been led to believe that drawing a child's attention to the type of person that a parent wants them to become is damaging to a child. Parents have been led to believe that drawing attention to the type of person a parent expects a child to become in the future will prompt a child experience him- or herself as somehow flawed, deficient, or lacking in the present. Parents have been led to believe that comparing the child's current behavior to a valued future state will damage a child's self-esteem, create feelings of shame and inadequacy, or otherwise stifle a child's sense of self.

Nothing can be further from the truth. Child-centered parents fear that holding out an image of the type of person a parent expects a child to become can damage a child's current sense of self. In fact, this very fear of damaging a child's self-esteem is most damaging to a child's sense of self because it can lead parents to protect children from the types of hardships that are inevitable in life and are necessary if children are to develop into competent, responsible, and caring adults. Instead of protecting children from possible feelings of inadequacy, it is the parent's job to arm children with the tools to cope with the hardships of that necessarily occur in life while simultaneously appreciating who one is at the present. This is part of what it means to cultivate character.

How can parents foster the process of self-cultivation in children without fear of infringing on their autonomy or damaging their self-esteem? The fact of the matter is that promoting self-cultivation in children actually enhances rather than diminishes autonomy and self-esteem. This is because self-cultivation fosters what psychologist Carol Dweck has called the growth rather than fixed mindset toward learning. As shown in Table 2.1, the fixed mindset consists of the belief that one's intelligence or ability is fixed and unchangeable; the growth mindset is the belief that one's intelligence and ability are changeable and develop through effort and perseverance. Children who hold a fixed mindset identify themselves with their presumed fixed abilities. Their self-esteem depends on the extent to which they can be seen as possessing valued talents and abilities. For children who think this way—and it is likely that many American children do—failure is a threat to self-esteem. If I strike out at baseball, I must be bad at baseball; if I get a poor grade in math, I must have low math ability. Because I believe there is nothing I can do to change my abilities, I adopt the strategy of avoiding tasks at which I think I might fail. To protect my self-esteem, I pursue easy tasks at which I know that I can excel.

Parents who consistently praise their children's abilities, protect children from hardship, and withhold corrective feedback out of a fear of hurting a child's self-esteem communicate a clear message to their children: your success comes from your inherent ability. If you do well at something, you should be proud of your ability. If you do poorly, the task is probably too difficult and extends beyond your ability. To press you further would run the risk of producing failure and feelings of shame. This message produces a suite of negative consequences. It fosters a preoccupation with protecting one's self-esteem rather

Table 2.1. Fixed and Growth Mindset Thinking

	Fixed Mindset Thinking (Proving My Inherent Worth)	Growth Mindset Thinking (Cultivating a Worthy Self)
Achievement	means proving that I'm already smart and have inherent talent.	means that I'm learning and developing new skills.
Being smart	means that I have inherent talent and make no mistakes.	is something that I make happen by working hard and confronting challenges.
Success	shows that I'm smart and have inherent abilities or talents.	is just one step on the road to mastering a new skill or becoming a better person; it is something to feel good about, but then it's important to take the next step.
Effort	means that I don't have natural ability.	is how new abilities and skills develop.
Feedback	is potentially threatening because it tells me whether I'm smart or dumb.	is not to be feared because it tells me what I have to do to improve my skills and abilities.
Mistakes	Produce a loss of self-esteem and confidence.	mean that I have not yet mastered what I'm trying to learn.
Failure	causes me to feel shame and embarrassment.	Means that I have to put in more effort to learn.
A poor grade	shows that I don't have an ability, and so I might as well simply give up.	means I have to work harder and continue to persevere until I learn.
Asking for help	means I have a weakness that I don't want to show people.	is a sign of strength and security; it means that I am not afraid to acknowledge areas in which I need to work harder; asking for help allows me to improve.
Successful peers	make me feel threatened and jealous.	inspire me.

than cultivating new abilities; it fails to arm children with the capacity to persevere through hardship; it fosters an attitude of praise-seeking on success and excuse-making in failure; it fails to promote skills for managing negative emotion and disappointment.

The child with a growth mindset does not believe her abilities are fixed; instead, she acts as if her abilities are cultivated over time through effort, hard work, and perseverance. The goals of a child with a fixed mindset are to present himself as capable by succeeding and avoid looking foolish by failing. In contrast, the goal of the child with a growth mindset is to cultivate her abilities. Whereas the child with a fixed mindset is motivated to do well in any particular task, the child with a growth mindset sees her success as a step in a longer process of mastering a new skill. More important, the child with a growth mindset experiences failure not as an indictment of her ability, but as indicating that more effort is needed to master the task. If the child believes that drawing ability develops over time through action and effort, then producing a poor drawing is merely an indication she has not yet learned to draw well. As a result, failure is not an inherent threat to a child's self-esteem.

Children who hold a fixed mindset identify themselves with their fixed abilities. Children who hold a growth mindset identify themselves with the process of cultivating new skills, abilities, and qualities. Thus, the child with the growth mindset is interested in learning to draw beautiful pictures, acquiring the ability to add, and getting feedback on whether she is learning well or poorly. In contrast the child with the fixed mindset is interested in gaining praise for a particular drawing, being praised for his ability to add, and getting an A on the test.

Virtues for Self-Cultivation

Parenting is not a morally neutral endeavor. If we want to foster the development of character in our children, we have to be willing to take a stand on the types of moral qualities we want them to acquire. Fostering character development in children thus involves identifying the virtues and values we want our children to cultivate and then helping children identify with and act on their understanding of these virtues.

The first step toward fostering children's character development is for parents to identify the virtues they want to promote in their children. These become their primary parenting goals. For example, if we want our children to become caring, responsible, and confident adults, then the parent's job becomes helping the child understand and identify him- or herself with these virtues. The parent essentially says: "Here are the qualities of a good person; this is how you cultivate these qualities. Now, I'll help you through this. Let's get to work."

Identifying Your Values and Virtues

Cultivating character involves identifying what virtues are important in life and making them part of one's central identity. Thus, the first step in the task of fostering character development is to articulate your own values and identify the virtues you want to promote in your child. Even though we may think that we know what type of person we want our child to become, the answers are not always clear. How do we choose what moral qualities we want to promote in our children? The Circle of Virtues (Figure I.2) contains a partial list of virtues. Which of these virtues do you find to be important and why?

One way to help clarify your system of values is to use the chart shown in Figure 2.1. This chart contains three concentric circles that you can use to identify virtues you feel are most important (center circle), moderately important (next circle), and less important (periphery) to foster in your child. Here is how to use it:

1. Write down names of your three most important virtues in the center circle; three moderately important

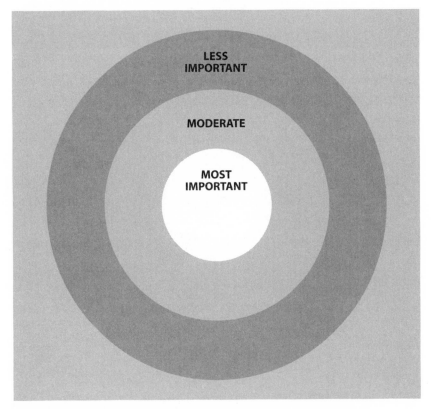

Figure 2.1. What Virtues Do You Value for Your Children?

virtues in the next outer ring; and three less important
virtues in the periphery.

2. Write the virtues down on the segment of circle according to how you think they go together. Place virtues
that you think are similar in some way next to each
other. Place those that are dissimilar further apart.

3. Circle groups of virtues that you think go together or
that are related in some important way.

4. Label each group of virtues. Briefly explain how you
think the virtues go together.

Figure 2.2 shows a sample chart completed by Mary, who
has three children. Mary identified love, care/compassion, and

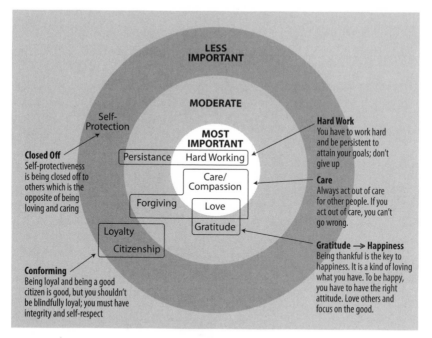

Figure 2.2. Sample Completed Virtue Chart

hard work as the virtues that she felt were most important; persistence, forgiveness, and gratitude as moderately important virtues; and self-protectiveness, loyalty, and citizenship as less important virtues. She grouped these virtues into three positive categories (care, gratitude, and hard work) and two negative ones (conforming and closed off). In describing each group of virtues, Mary was able to clarify some of the reasons she valued some over others.

Parents who engage in this activity are often surprised at the insights they gain into their own value systems. Identifying the values that guide our parenting is a simple process. Some find their values changing during the very process of reflecting on them. This shows that our values are not fixed things—they can and do change over time as we encounter new parenting experiences and reflect on the significance of those experiences.

Reversing the Entitlement Trend

As discussed in the introduction to this book, child-centered parenting tends to create a culture of entitlement in children. Although it is their intent to raise independent, confident, and proactive children, child-centered parents tend to raise kids who are entitled, self-focused, undisciplined, and lacking in moral purpose. An authoritative commitment to the cultivation of character is necessary as a corrective to the corrosive effects of child-centered parenting. Although parents are the ultimate arbiters of the virtues that they seek to inculcate in their children, several virtues stand out as particularly important if we are to reverse the culture of entitlement that we have witnessed over the past decades. These include the virtues of mastery, perseverance, emotional management, and concern for others.

Mastery

Mastery is the idea that learning and self-cultivation are long-term processes that involve acquiring comprehensive control over skills and knowledge in some area of life. Someone has achieved a degree of mastery when he gains expertise in relatively broad areas of learning. The power of mastery is expressed in the story of the three masons.

There once was a traveler who journeyed around globe in search of wisdom. He happened upon a village where came upon a large commotion. Approaching the nearest laborer, he asked, "Excuse me. May I ask what's going on?" The laborer replied curtly, "Can't you see? I'm laying bricks." The traveler approached a second laborer with the same question. The mason replied, "Can't you see? I'm earning a living to support my family." Finally, the traveler posed the question to a third laborer. With a broad smile and a gleam in his eye, the mason replied with great pride: "Can't you see? We're building a cathedral."

When a parent begins to think of parenting goals in terms of promoting mastery, her entire approach to parenting can become transformed. In promoting self-cultivation in a child, the parent's goal is to help the child think like the third mason. Rather than building a cathedral, goal of the child is to build a self. The parent's job is to help her child master the skills and knowledge the child needs to become his or her best self.

Mastering a skill (or building a self) is different than completing a task. Take, for example, the case of homework. Martha and Juana are parents of two different children. Martha's goal is to have her son complete his homework. In contrast, Juana's goal is to help her daughter master addition. How might these two parents approach the problem of supervising their children's homework? Martha's attention is focused on the task—getting the work done. She can meet her goal in many ways: she can ask if the work has been completed, check to see if it has been done right, or work with her son to help him complete the homework correctly. All of these are good strategies.

Juana, however, wants her child master the skill of adding. She understands that the assigned homework is merely a task—a step along the road of mastering addition. Her mindset is different from Martha's. Juana wants to make sure that her child knows how to add. As a result, Juana is more likely to work with her child to find out what she knows and doesn't know. She will make sure that she understands how to do each problem. But she is unlikely to stop there. She may teach her child different strategies for performing the same problems; show her child how to apply her adding skills to different problems; go backward to fill a gap in her child's knowledge; move forward to the next step in learning addition, and so forth.

Martha simply wants to get the task done; she is teaching her son to lay bricks. Juana wants her child to master addition; she is teaching her child to build a cathedral. Fostering self-cultivation means helping children identify the goals of their own development and then helping persevere en route to getting there.

Perseverance

Perseverance is the capacity to devote the level of sustained effort and emotional control needed to cultivate any given skill or understanding. For a long time, we have erroneously believed that individual differences in cognitive ability explain why some people are able to accomplish more in life than others do. However, cognitive ability is simply inert without the motivational and emotional capacities to direct one's abilities, sustain them, and persevere en route to cultivating new skills and abilities over time. People who are able to sustain their effort over time are much more likely to succeed than those who do not. Research shows that hard work, effort, and perseverance are more important determinants of achievement than intelligence.

Promoting perseverance in children requires a certain attitude toward development. The situations that call for perseverance are not necessarily pleasant. A child may not want to continue working on a difficult homework assignment, clean up her room, or wait to leave the dinner table. Three obstacles tend to prevent parents from teaching their children the virtues of perseverance and task mastery. First, parents dislike seeing their children struggle. They typically do not wish to see themselves as the cause of their children's distress. For many parents, loving their children means making them feel good, not bad. Acting out of empathy and love, parents respond to a child's frustration and emotional distress by removing the source of the distress, rather than teaching the child to persevere and solve the problem at hand. This would happen, for example, if a parent, observing her child struggle and complain, were to excuse the child from completing a difficult homework assignment. This, however, teaches the child how to avoid rather than confront the realities of the problems that lie before him.

Second, parents may believe that expecting children to persevere through difficulty may undermine a child's autonomy or independence. From this view, a parent may see it as a child's right to choose whether she wants to complete a difficult assignment, leave the table when she wants, or clean up her room. To be sure, parents may grant children the right to control particular areas of their lives. However, there is a danger in treating children as if they were little adults who have the capacity to make good choices on their own. Children are incomplete beings. They not only know less than their parents, they cannot anticipate the long-term results of their choices as well as adults can. It is a mistake to grant children the capacity to choose not to develop skills that are valued by a more knowledgeable and responsible parent.

Third, and perhaps most important, parents may fear that even if children persevere in the context of a difficultly, they may still fail. Such failure would then undermine the child's confidence and self-esteem. This often motivates parents to adopt an "effort is more important than achievement" mentality. It is not uncommon to hear parents say, "all that matters is that you do your best" or "you don't have to be the first; all I ask is that you give your best effort." This way of thinking can actually undermine the development of persistence. Sometimes, people mistake the growth mindset as suggesting that effort is more important than achievement. This is not the case. The growth mindset states that effort and perseverance foster incremental achievement, that effort and persistence are the vehicles of achievement. To cultivate a mindset of persistence, it is necessary to guide children through the learning process and show how effort and persistence leads to better learning—even if progress is modest. Of course, over time, modest gains have a habit of turning into major advances.

Self-Regulation and Emotional Management

Perseverance through to mastery is not possible without struggle. Aristotle said that one of the main things parents can teach their children is a proper attitude toward pleasure and pain. This is an extraordinary statement: not all pleasures are good; not all pains are bad. If this is so, then parents must teach children that some pleasures are to be cultivated and others avoided; some pains should be endured in the service of some greater good. We want our children to cultivate the pleasure of helping a friend but avoid the pleasure of choosing play over homework. Similarly, although we want to teach our children to avoid the pain of touching a hot stove, we want to encourage them to endure the struggle that is required to learn new things. To develop a proper attitude toward struggle, parents must be willing to teach their children how to manage difficult emotion in the pursuit of worthwhile goals.

American parents value autonomy, independence, and self-confidence in their children. As already discussed, several generations of parents have been led to believe that children's learning should be self-directed and internally motivated. A corollary to this idea is that learning should be fun. If children are naturally curious beings, they will learn best when what they are learning excites their interests. Based on this type of thinking, parents and educators alike have adopted the strategy of creating learning activities that capitalize on the interests of children. Thus, rather than setting high-maturity demands that children are expected to meet, many parents and teachers modify their demands to match the child's interests. As a result, parents and educators have failed to provide the kind of emotional and behavioral guidance that is necessary for children to develop the capacity for emotional and behavioral regulation.[1]

Unfortunately, not all learning is fun. As children get older, learning requires sustained effort, perseverance, and a capacity

---

1. Over the past decade or so, student-centered teaching has begun to give way to the new emphasis on accountability in education. The desire for accountability has spawned a culture of high-stakes testing for students and teachers alike. Teachers are expected to hold children to a common set of educational standards. Workloads, including homework, have increased. Despite these changes, U.S. students still fare poorly compared to other technologically developed nations of the world. A solution to these educational problems remains elusive. However, part of the problem likely relates to our collective failure to foster an appropriate attitude toward perseverance, mastery, and struggle in our children, our families, and our schools.

for managing difficult emotions over time. These are the very skills that many children fail to develop. As aspects of moral character, the ability to sustain attention and manage difficult emotion requires steady and deliberate guidance from more accomplished others. In development, the capacity to regulate one's own actions and emotions moves from "regulation with others" → "self-regulation." Children first acquire the ability to regulate their emotions and behavior in their social interactions with others; later they are able regulate their feelings and actions for themselves.

Concern for Others

All of us have at least two categories of motives: self-interest and concern for others. People act out of self-interest when they pursue food out of hunger and thirst, pursue their own personal goals, seek fame and fortune, and so on. We act out of concern for others when offer assistance, share food, console someone in distress, or otherwise act for the benefit of other people. A concern for another is the basis of all forms of moral conduct.

When children are very young, self-interest and concern for others tend to occur in separate situations. In some situations, children act on their own self-interests; in others, they care for the visible needs of other people. For example, in one situation, if Todd wants to play with Lexi's doll, he may simply grab it from her. On a different occasion, if Todd sees Lexi cry over a broken toy, he might attempt to comfort her, fix the toy for her, or give her another toy. Children tend to switch from self-interest to concern for others from moment to moment.

Over time, children's self-interests will naturally come into conflict with the interests of others. Part of cultivating moral character is teaching children to become aware of the needs and interests of others (e.g., "Look what happened when you grabbed Lexi's doll. How do you think that made her feel?"), care about those interests (e.g., "How would you feel if she took your doll? Is that how you want to make her feel?"), and ultimately coordinate their own interests with those of others (e.g., "I know that you want to play with Lexi's doll. But she is playing with it right now. What can you do to get a turn with the doll without just taking it from Lexi and making her sad?")

Through hundreds of interactions like this, morally sensitive children come to reconcile their self-interest with their feelings of concern for others. Over time, moral character develops as a result of *identifying oneself with one's concern for others*. Morally exemplary children *care* about other people; they make care of others an important (but by no means exclusive) part of their self-interest. They tend to be those who achieve a sense of satisfaction out of the act of being caring to others. Instead of seeing concern for others as something that is at odds with self-interest, morally exemplary teens experience caring about others as an expression of who they are. In so doing, they will have forged a moral identity and will become more likely to act out of a sense of *purpose* rather than simply out of a sense of self-interest.

APPLY DISCIPLINE INSTEAD OF PUNISHMENT

Rewards and punishments are ineffective strategies for fostering compliance and long-term moral growth.

==

Most parents yearn for harmonious relationships with their children. As parents, we often struggle with the balance between loving our children and providing them with direction and discipline. We often see loving support as the opposite of discipline. However, this sort of thinking causes problems. Parents who emphasize love over discipline tend to have the most conflict with their children. This is because parents who are responsive but not demanding tend to produce children who are demanding but not responsive! As a result, parents who seek the most harmonious relationships with their children frequently have the most discordant ones.

It is possible to cultivate harmonious and collaborative relationships with children over time. However, this typically requires that parents set the terms of the authoritative parent–child relationship early in development. This not only means providing children with plenty of warmth, affection, and support, it also means not being afraid to assert the legitimate authority that comes with being a responsible parent. It is important to keep in mind that authoritative parenting is not the same as authoritarian parenting. Authoritarian parents are coercive; they set and enforce rules without sensitivity to their children's needs, experiences, and skills. Authoritative parents enforce maturity demands while simultaneously being responsive to their children's needs.

Harmonious relationships between children and parents develop and become more nuanced and sophisticated over time. However, they cannot develop without the parent first establishing an initial foundation of parental authority in the relationship. This chapter describes concepts and strategies for establishing an initial foundation of control early within the parent–child relationship. In later chapters, we examine how to build on this initial foundation to build increasingly cooperative and collaborative relationships with children that promote their autonomy while simultaneously preserving parental authority.

Discipline Is Not the Same as Punishment

When we think of parental authority, perhaps the first thing we think of is the question of discipline. The term *discipline* is a highly charged word. People use it to refer to different things — instruction, consequences, punishment, "time out," and so on. At base, however, the term *discipline* refers to a type of instruction given to people en route to mastering some skill, field, or area. A person has discipline when he is able to control his behavior in ways that allow him to function within a given field or area of endeavor. We even call the various fields or areas in which people cultivate skills *disciplines*. The fields of chemistry, biology, psychology, and engineering are examples of disciplines.

When it comes to parenting, it is helpful to think of discipline in a similar way. To discipline a child is to help that child cultivate discipline — that is, the capacity to control his or her behavior in terms of some sort of rule system. When we discipline a child, we instruct the child about how to cultivate the capacity to control his or her behavior. We discipline to help the child cultivate self-discipline. From this perspective, disciplining a child becomes anything that we do to inculcate self-discipline in the child.

Thinking of discipline in this broader way frees us from the common view that discipline is the same as punishment. It isn't. We tend to think that we are being irresponsible unless we follow children's misdeeds with some form of punishment. However, punishment is not the only way to discipline a child. More important, punishment is not an *effective* way to discipline children. The simple fact of the matter is that punishment doesn't work. Happily, it is possible to cultivate discipline in children in ways that do not involve punishment. There are many ways to be an authoritative parent without having to resort to punishment. It may require some rethinking about how we approach parenting.

Why Punishment Doesn't Work

Perhaps the most common way of thinking about discipline is the old and clunky theory of reward and punishment. The thinking is simple enough: reward the behavior you want, and punish the behavior you don't want. Before moving on, let's become clear about what these terms mean. By punishment, I simply mean the practice of administering an unwanted or unpleasant external consequence to someone (e.g., a child) for having engaged in an unwanted action. The theory of punishment is based on the idea that if someone knows that he will receive something unpleasant for engaging in some behavior, he will refrain from engaging in that behavior.

This approach to discipline is simple, common, and just plain ineffective.

It takes only a few moments of reflection to prove this to yourself. Consider the following. You are driving on the highway, a bit over the speed limit. (Okay, maybe more than just a bit). In front of you, you see a police cruiser on the side of the road. Your heart jumps a bit. Your foot touches the brakes and you slow down. You pass the police officer unscathed. Whew! You feel grateful, and just a little bit afraid of what could have been. So you start driving more slowly . . . for about a minute and a half.

Let's change the scenario. Same situation—except, as you pass the police officer, you see his lights start flashing. The officer starts his vehicle and pulls you over. You get a ticket. You put the ticket in the glove compartment. This time you really do slow down . . . for about seven minutes.

Let's change the scenario one more time. Same situation. You get pulled over and get a ticket. But this time it is a ticket for $50,000. They take away your license for a full year. You pay the $50,000. At great inconvenience, you take the subway to work for the next year. A year later, you get your license back! And you never speed again.

What does this story tell us about punishment? Well, it suggests exactly what decades of research tell us.

Does punishment "work"? It depends on what you mean by "work." If you mean, "Does punishment stop unwanted behavior?," the answer is "yes"—but only in two types of circumstances. First, punishment stops unwanted behavior when the punishing agent is present. This occurs, for example, when a speeding driver sees the police officer. The driver slows down out of a fear of punishment. The threat of punishment causes the driver to slow down and drive within the speed limit. However, once the person has driven past the police officer—and the punishing agent is no longer present—the driver is back up to her former speed.

The second set of circumstances occurs when the punishment is so severe, so intense, that it is seriously debilitating in some way. A person receiving a $50,000 ticket and a year's suspension from driving would be so severely pained that she would never speed again.

Thus, punishment stops unwanted behavior only in the short term, when the punisher is present, or if the punishment is so severe as to be debilitating. Few parents will find either one of these circumstances to be acceptable. It is not possible for a punisher (or the threat of punishment) to be present all the time, or even during those times when a child is likely to engage in some unwanted behavior. Even if it were, such a practice would be undesirable. As parents, we do not simply want our children to refrain from unwanted behavior in the short run; we want them to do so in the long term. We do not simply want our children to refrain from unwanted behavior (e.g., drawing on the walls, grabbing a toy from a playmate), we want them to engage in wanted behavior (e.g., drawing on paper, making requests from playmates). Punishment does nothing to bring about these desired long-term outcomes.

Of course, with respect to the second option—debilitating punishment—we do not want to bring harm to our children. Compliance to rules at the cost of serious pain is simply unacceptable. Even if parents were willing to punish children severely, the effects of harsh and abusive parenting are severe and long-lasting.

Punishment is not an effective disciplinary strategy.

Punishment from a Child's Perspective

Another way to understand why punishment is an ineffective child management strategy is to examine it from the perspective of the child. Imagine that you have asked seven-year-old Tommy to clean up his toys. Tommy is reluctant. He ignores your request and simply continues to play. In situations like this, parents often resort to threats and punishments. For example, a parent might say, "If you don't clean up those toys right now, there will be no dessert tonight." (Feel free to replace this particular threat with any other threat that comes to mind.)

Might this threat motivate Tommy to clean up his toys? As suggested above, yes—the threat of punishment can work, in the short run, if the person doling out the punishment is present, and if the child cares about the punishment. However, even under these circumstances, the threat of punishment often fails. Let's examine why.

In any disciplinary encounter, it is always helpful to ask: What are the child's interests? What are Tommy's interests? Tommy wants to play with his toy. He doesn't want to clean up his toys. It's no wonder why the request to clean up is a difficult for Tommy—everything is stacked against him! If he decides to clean up his toys, he has to stop having fun (–) and do something that is not fun (–). If he decides to keep playing, he gets to continue to have fun (+), and avoid something unpleasant (+)! Given this situation, how might a parent motivate Tommy? His mother used the strategy of threatening punishment. How might Tommy experience the threat of punishment? First, the punishment is something that has not yet occurred. If it occurs, it is going to occur later—in the fuzzy future.

Young children are concrete beings. It is often difficult for them to imagine what's going to happen two minutes into the future. Here we have the parent asking the child to imagine a bad thing that may happen "after dinner. The future is fuzzy and unclear. However, the present is happening right now.

Here is Tommy's choice:

> If I stop playing (–) and clean up (–), I'll be miserable right now (– –),
> but I'll get dessert sometime in the fuzzy, hard to imagine future (+)
> If I play (+) and avoid cleaning up (+), I'll be happy now (++),
> but I *may* not get dessert in the fuzzy, hard to imagine future (–).

For Tommy, the fun that he gets from playing with his toys is happening now; the misery of having to clean up his toys is happening now. Not getting dessert, however, is something might happen in the future. Imagining the fuzzy future is less motivating than experiencing the passionate present.

It is always important to look at any disciplinary situation from the point of view of the child. Putting ourselves in the child's position can help us understand the child's experience or even experience what the child is experiencing. When we do this, we gain greater insight into what motivates the child to act the way he does. In the case of punishment, we can begin to see that unless it is severe or continuously looming—, the threat of punishment is a weak deterrent to unwanted behavior. Children who willingly and fearlessly comply with their parents do so for reasons that have little to do with the threat of punishment. We explore these reasons in more detail in coming chapters.

Why Rewards Don't Work

After we come to appreciate the ineffectiveness of punishment, the next question becomes, "what about rewards?" Even when they use it, parents instinctively seem to find punishment distasteful. Punishment seems negative. So what about rewards? Rewards aren't negative; they are positive, and we hear so much about "positive parenting."

The theory of reward is the opposite of the theory of punishment. To reward a child is to provide him or her with some wanted external consequence in response to producing some desirable action. The theory of reward is based on the idea that children will engage in behaviors that they might not otherwise perform if they know they will receive some wanted outcome from it. This, of course, is the logic we use in the workplace. People do not choose to work for free; they work because they know that they are going to get a paycheck at the end of the week. Rewards work in the workplace. If we stopped receiving a paycheck, work would come to an abrupt halt.

When children exhibit behavior problems, clinical psychologists often suggest arranging a reward schedule for the child. This frequently takes the form of checklists or sticker charts that can be turned into attractive prizes for children. Imagine that eight-year-old Will is uncooperative at home. He engages in backtalk, refuses to come to the table when called, and takes too long to get out of the house in the morning. A clinician might suggest identifying a series of alternative behaviors that his parents want Will to perform, and then giving Will a sticker each time he performs the behavior. Will can earn stickers each time he says, "Okay, Mom," rather than giving backtalk, comes to the table when called, and is ready to leave the house on time each morning. Let us also imagine that Will is highly motivated to cooperate because he is desperate for a new video game. In these circumstances, it is entirely possible that, if his parents were consistent, Will would increase the number of times he says "Okay, Mom," comes to the table when called, and gets out of the house on time in the morning. Putting him on a reward schedule might well have the desired effect.

The problem, of course, is the same that we encounter in the case of punishment. External rewards motivate behavior only in the short run, as long as the reward program is in effect, and only as long as the child is already motivated to obtain the reward. If we take away the reward system, the child, just like the worker who fails to receive a paycheck, will typically stop performing the desired behavior. Furthermore, when the child complies in the context of the promise of reward, he is behaving to receive the reward; he does not choose to perform the act willingly. For example, when his mother makes a request, rather than talking back, Will might say, "okay, Mom," to gain a sticker that he can turn into a prize. But he does not say "okay, Mom" out of respect for his mother as an act of cooperation. Unless Will internalizes the rule or reason for saying "okay, Mom," his compliance will be short-lived.[1]

---

1. It is possible, during the time that the child is placed on a reward schedule, to teach him or her rules and reasons to comply with the rule in the long run. For example, a parent might accompany her administration of rewards by saying something like, "do you see what happens when you say, 'okay, Mom'? The job gets done faster and we are all happy." Over time, the child may internalize these rules, which can lead to long-term compliance. However, this does not suggest the effectiveness of rewards. Instead, it shows their limitations.

Thus, external rewards and punishments are ineffective to ensure rule following in the long run. At best, they are only effective in the short term while the reward or punishment systems are consistently in place. Furthermore, even in the short term, external rewards are effective only to the extent that children value those rewards over the pleasures they may receive from everyday rule-violating behavior. Similarly, even in the short term, punishments only deter behavior to the extent that the child experiences or evaluates the punishment as sufficiently unpleasant or unwanted.

What Works?

This raises the obvious question: what *does* work? Again, what do we mean by "work"? By "work," I mean the goal of promoting responsible behavior in the long run. Hundreds of studies on children and parents point to the same general conclusion. The most effective strategies for producing long-term rule compliance are those that lead to the internalization of parental values. These include the following.

Clear Limit Setting

Setting limits simply means having standards for what a child is permitted to do and not permitted to do. Effective parents have high standards for their children. Limit setting is a form of high standards. When we create rules and set limits—you have to say "please" when you ask for something, homework first, you can play only within the yard, bedtime is 10 pm, be home by 9 pm—we are defining the areas for which we want our children to assume responsibility. But simply having limits is

---

Without additional motivation to internalize reasons for rule following, once the reward system has been lifted, the child's unwanted behaviors are likely to return.

not enough—. We have to enforce them in meaningful ways. How do we do this?

Explanation and Dialogue

It makes no sense to have a long negotiation with your child about the rules. You are the one setting the rules (although they can be flexible, given circumstances). However, we can explain the basis of the rules to our children. Research on the development of the internalization of rules is unequivocal. Children are more likely to internalize a rule if their parents explain the reasons for it. Here are some examples of explanations: "Don't hit your sister! That hurts her! How would you feel if she were to hit you?"; "We don't write on the walls. It makes the walls messy and then you have to clean them. Instead, we write with crayon and paper"; "I want you in by 10 pm because I am worried about you driving late at night. I want you safe at home, and you need your sleep."

Sometimes, parents are suspect of explanation as a discipline strategy. They may say, "I can explain a rule to my child, but that doesn't mean she will follow it!" That is correct! Explanation simply clarifies the rule. For some children, a clear explanation is all that is needed. For most children, however, other strategies may be needed to enforce the rule.

Meaningful Consequences

A meaningful consequence can sound a lot like a punishment. But there is a big difference. With punishment, we give a child some unpleasant experience to make him or her stop behaving in some way. With meaningful consequences, a child takes responsibility for the unwanted outcomes of his own actions. A child who writes on the walls is not sent to his room; he may be directed clean the walls instead, and his crayons might be taken away unless he promises to use them only with paper. A child who refuses to eat dinner may be told that she will not get dinner later (and thus that she will have to wait until the next morning for her next meal). A child who cannot get home by 10 pm must demonstrate in concrete ways that she can be trusted in performing similar activities before she will be allowed to go out again. Punishments are the arbitrary pairing of pain with some unwanted behavior; meaningful consequences link a child's behavior to the broken rule in a meaningful way. We have much more to say about meaningful consequences in Key 4.

A Mutually Responsive Parent–Child Relationship

The most important resource that you have to influence your child is your relationship with him or her. A healthy relationship is one in which a parent enforces high expectations in the context of clear and loving communication. High expectations are needed to set a direction for the child; warmth and nurturance are needed to make the relationship work. Children who have healthy relationships with their parents come to see that their parents can be helpful—even through adolescence.

Authoritative Discipline in Five Easy Steps

Four-year old Noah wants the teddy bear that his sister Lauren is playing with. He asks her, "Can I have the teddy?" When Lauren says, "I'm not done yet!" Noah grabs the bear from his sister. Lauren begins to cry.

Eight-year-old Elizabeth is done playing with her trains. She leaves her trains in the living room and goes into the kitchen for a snack. Her mother asks her to pick up her toys and put them away. Elizabeth says, "In a minute! I'm hungry." Twenty minutes later, Elizabeth's mom finds the toys right where Elizabeth left them: in the middle of the living room.

Eleven-year-old Sadie won't do her math homework. When asked whether she has any math homework, she denies it. "Ms. Denny didn't give us any today." "I did my homework in school." "We didn't have math today." But when you check her backpack, you find her math homework. In addition to not doing her homework, Sadie is lying.

These are everyday problems that most parents face at one time or another. Quite frankly, how we respond to any single problem on any given day is not going to make or break a child's development. All parents are going to lose their temper from time to time. All parents are going to give in to their children's unreasonable requests at one time or another. Don't beat yourself up for that! Instead, realize that it is the way we respond to children over time that matters—it's the pattern that counts.

Authoritative parents have high expectations for the children while simultaneously being sensitive and responsive to their children's interests and needs. How does this translate into effective discipline? Most of the time, everyday misbehaviors can be handled in five easy steps. These steps are described and illustrated in Figure 3.1.

Step 1: Identify (and Stop)
the Unwanted Behavior

This is the obvious first step. Identify the unwanted behavior and call the child's attention to it. It is not effective simply to tell the child to "stop." Although it may be very clear to you, it is often not clear to the child what the unwanted behavior is. Rather than simply, "Stop that," say, "Don't grab the teddy bear! Give it back right now!" "I see that you have not yet picked up the toys from the living room." "You said that you have no math homework, but here is the math homework that your teacher sent home."

STEP	EXAMPLE	WHAT THIS DOES
1. **Stop** the unwanted behavior.	*Don't grab that!*	Stops unwanted behavior and gets child's attention
2. **Acknowledge** the child's legitimate interests	*I know you want to play with the Teddy Bear…*	Helps child feel understood while also helping child understand his own motives for misbehaving
3. **State** and **explain** the **rule** the child violated.	*We never grab. Grabbing without asking shows you don't care that someone else is using the toy. How would you feel if I grabbed the Teddy Bear from you when you were playing with it?*	Establishes clear limits on child's behavior and explains the reasons for those limits. Child learns adult's reasons for establishing the rule and also learns why it is in his own interest to comply with the rule.
4. Provide **interest-relevant** consequences if necessary.	*Now give me the Teddy Bear. You will not be allowed to play with the Teddy Bear until you are able to ask politely and wait your turn.*	Because the child wants the bear, taking it away is personally meaningful to the child. Requiring correct behavior to get the wanted bear teaches and motivates compliance.
5. Provide **alternative behaviors** that the child can use to advance his interests	*Now, let's try it. If you want the Teddy Bear, you first ask, "Can I play with Teddy when you are done?"… Good. Now, you'll have to wait until I'm done washing him. If you are able to wait that long without whining, you'll get the bear. If not, we are going to have to start over.*	This step teaches the child to replace an unwanted behavior with a wanted behavior. Because the child wants the bear, he is already motivated to learn how to get it. We rarely learn new behaviors just by being told. Guiding the child through the actual wanted behavior is the best way to teach it.

Figure 3.1. Authoritative Discipline in Five Easy Steps

Step 2: Acknowledge the Child's Legitimate Interests

All people act on the basis of their interests. Any person's behavior is a way of advancing their interests—their goals, motives, desires, and so forth. As long as our behavior works for us—(continues to advance our interests) we will continue to behave the same way. However, when our behavior stops working for us—when it no longer leads to its intended outcome—we will be motivated to change our behavior.

There are several reasons it is important to identify and acknowledge the interests that motivate a child's behavior. First, if we want to modify children's behavior, we have to identify the legitimate interests that motivate that behavior. Then we can teach the child alternative and more appropriate ways of advancing his or her interests. Most often, children's behavior is motivated by interests that have some degree of positive intention. For example, a child who grabs a teddy bear is motivated by the desire to play with the teddy bear. In this example, there is nothing wrong with wanting the teddy bear; there is only something wrong with grabbing it as a way to obtain it! The child who leaves her toys in the middle of the living room is motivated by a desire to avoid the displeasure of putting effort into picking up the toys. That is certainly an understandable motive. The child will have to learn to deal with her displeasure, we can certainly understand why she would not want to pick up her toys. A child who avoids and lies about math homework is, mostly likely, afraid of facing something difficult. Perhaps she experiences the math as too hard, is ashamed of her inability to perform, or is having difficulty with her math teacher.

The second reason it is important to acknowledge the interests that motivate misbehavior has to do with its role in building the parent–child relationship. We all want to be understood. One of the most painful experiences we have is the feeling of not being heard and not being understood. This is one of the reasons children will give excuses for bad behavior—"yeah, but she wouldn't give me the teddy bear!" To acknowledge the child's interests communicates that you understand the child's (legitimate) interests and that you are on the side of advancing those legitimate interests. A child who learns that you care about his or her interests will learn to trust you and will be motivated to listen to what you have to say.

Thus, after identifying the problem behavior, it is important for parents to acknowledge their child's legitimate interests: "I know you want to play with the teddy bear . . . "; "It's never fun to have to pick up after yourself . . . "; or "Sometimes, we encounter things that are really hard for us, and we try to avoid them . . . " But then, of course, there's a "but."

Step 3: State and Explain the Rule the Child Violated

The third step is to identify the rule that the child has violated and explain the reasons for the rule. This is the point at which the parent gets to advance his or her interests, standards, values and rules.

This is a very important step. Hundreds of studies on child development support the idea that the only long-term process that leads to long term change in behavior is the internalization of rules. Long-term behavior change occurs when children take parental rules, internalize them, and make them their own. This is a process that itself takes long periods of time. One of the most important things that parents can do to foster rule internalization is to explain the basis of the rules they are attempting to enforce. Like adults, when children understand the reasons for a rule, they are more likely to accept the rule and follow it. The best way to explain a rule is to focus on the effects of the unwanted behavior both for the child him- or herself and for other people. Here are some examples:

> *"We never grab! Grabbing tells your sister that you don't care that she is playing with the teddy bear. When*

you grab, you hurt her feelings. How would you feel if she grabbed the toy from you when you were playing with it? If you just grab toys from people, no one is going to want to play with you."

"When you leave your toys in the middle of the room, then someone else has to clean them up for you. That someone is often me. You know how you feel when you have to clean up toys? Well I feel the same way! Do you really want make me do your work for you? What do you think other people think of you when you just leave your things around the house?

"My dear, when you lie to me about your homework, so many bad things can happen. First, if you lie—whatever the reason—that means I can't help you. If you are having problems with math, they are not going to go away! You will need help to get through them. I'm here to help, but I can't help if you don't tell me. Worse, when you lie, that tells me that I can't trust what you say. And when that happens. . ."

Step 4: Provide Personally Meaningful Consequences, If Needed

The fourth step is to arrange for personally meaningful consequences for a child's misbehavior, if necessary. A personally meaningful consequence is not a punishment, a time out, or anything like that. Punishments are not personally meaningful consequences. Punishment is based on the simple (and flawed) idea that people will stop doing something if it becomes associated with something unpleasant.

A personally meaningful consequence is something different. A personally meaningful consequence is one that is directly relevant to the child's immediate and long-term interests. Remember, as long as our behavior advances our interests, we will be motivated to continue to behave in the same way. When our behavior does not advance our interests, we are motivated to change it. A personally meaningful consequence is one that stops the child's behavior from advancing his or her interests.

For example, a child grabs a toy from his sister. When the parent takes the toy away from him, he will learn that grabbing doesn't work. A child avoids picking up her toys by saying that she will clean up her toys after she has her snack. If the parent says, "you get no snack until you pick up your toys," the child will learn that her delaying strategy will fail. If a child lies to get out of doing homework, requiring that the lie be followed up with the homework (and perhaps even more work) will show that lies (when one gets caught) don't work.

Arranging for personally meaningful consequences for a child's behavior goes a long way toward motivating that child to modify his or her behavior. All by itself, personally meaningful consequences are insufficient. They basically say grabbing, delaying, or lying are not going to pay off for you. These behaviors will not advance your interests. Though these are important messages, they do not communicate the most important message. Although they teach children what will *not* advance his or her interests, they do not teach alternative behaviors that *will* advance their interests.

Step 5: Provide Alternative Behaviors That Child Can Use to Advance His or Her Interests Appropriately

Effective discipline teaches children to respect the limits you place on their behavior. However, for a disciplinary strategy to produce long-term results, it should not only teach children what not to do, it must also teach them what they can and should do. People act on the basis of their interests. Unless children internalize parental rules or otherwise see it in their interest to follow those rules, they are unlikely to conform to those rules.

If children behave on the basis of their interests, they also misbehave on the basis of their interests. One powerful way to modify children's misbehaviors is to teach them alternative and appropriate ways to advance their interests. A child who grabs a toy from his sister is already motivated by his interest to play with the toy. As a result, he is already motivated to learn an alternative, appropriate, and more effective way to obtain the toy. He is thus ready to be shown that asking politely and waiting one's turn will likely be more effective than simply grabbing the toy.

A child who attempts to avoid an unwanted task by saying she will do it after her snack is playing on her parent's sympathies. She has two interests in this situation: avoid picking up her toys and having her snack. In this case, the parent can use one of her child's interests in the service the other. "If you want your snack, you are going to have to pick up your toys first. If you don't want to pick up your toys, you are not going to be able to play in the living room." (This will be discussed in greater detail in Key 4.)

A child who lies in an attempt to avoid difficult homework must not only be shown that lying will not help her solve that problem; she must also be shown an alternative behavior that will solve her problem. This can be done in several ways. Once the lie is exposed and the homework is found, the parents can work with the child to help her work through the homework successfully and cope with the anxiety and fear that she experiences when confronting her work. By helping the child articulate her fear about homework, her parents can teach her that asking for help is a better solution to her problem than avoiding her homework through lying.

Task 3.1. Practicing Authoritative Discipline

It's one thing to know that we should discipline without punishment; it's quite another thing to put it into practice. Give yourself the time to develop new ways disciplining your child. One way to start the process is to practice beforehand. Think of some common misbehaviors that you tend to see in your children. Write the problem on the chart below. What strategies can you think of for the steps described on the chart? (Keys 4 and 8 can also help you find strategies for some of the steps.)

AUTHORITATIVE DISCIPLINE PRACTICE SHEET

CHILD'S MISBEHAVIOR:

STEP	WHAT TO DO
1. **Stop** the unwanted behavior.	
2. **Acknowledge** the child's **feelings** and **legitimate Interests.**	
3. **State** the **rule** the child violated and explain to the child concretely why it is important.	
4. Provide **personally meaningful** ("interest-relevant") consequences, if necessary.	
5. Show an **alternative behavior** that can advance the child's interests in an appropriate way.	

What about "Just Deserts"?

You now may be convinced that punishment is an ineffective discipline strategy. You may even be convinced that there are effective alternatives to punishment. However, you might still be skeptical about giving up punishment entirely. There are several reasons parents may find it difficult to abandon punishment. First, it is one thing to say there are alternatives to punishment. However, it is not until parents actually experience success with these alternative methods that they will be completely convinced. This takes time and practice. This is an understandable source of reluctance.

A second source of reluctance has to do with the difficult issue of "just deserts." Up until this point, the primary objection to punishment has been that it simply doesn't work. However, a parent might say, "That's all fine and good. But even if it doesn't work, children still need to be punished when they misbehave. They need to pay a penalty for having done something wrong." From this perspective, punishment is not simply about stopping unwanted behavior in the future—it is also about balancing the moral scales. If someone does something wrong, he should get his just deserts. This is a strong moral argument, one that is separate and distinct from the issue of whether punishment is effective. This way of thinking has a long history. It is deeply ingrained in the way we think about right and wrong and is, of course, the basis of our legal system. If a person commits a crime, she should suffer a penalty, subject to the constraint that the punishment fit the crime. Such feelings are understandable.

For those who feel this way, I suggest a simple thought experiment. What do we want when we want people to get their just deserts? If I am hurt, I want the person who hurt me to feel what I feel. If someone steals from me, I want that person to suffer in a way that is proportional to my suffering. If someone betrays me, I want that person to feel what it feels like to be betrayed. When we are wronged, we want retribution—we want to balance the moral scales.

There are many ways to balance the moral scales after a wrongdoing. Imagine I am late in picking you up for your appointment. You explain how my actions have affected you. You feel uncared for, disrespected, and hurt. Because of my lateness, you have missed your appointment. Imagine now that I am changed by your words. I appreciate your experience in ways that I had failed to before. I have a genuine feeling of remorse. I apologize sincerely and ask your forgiveness. You sense my sincerity and forgive me. In this situation, although it is impossible to repair the practical situation (the missed appointment), it is possible to repair the moral imbalance between us. If am genuinely remorseful, you may forgive me. If you do, it will be because you truly believe that I appreciate that I carry the burden of your pain and intend to do better in the future.

This example shows that it is possible to balance the moral scales without retribution. When we are wronged, we want the wrong to be acknowledged and repaired. When I apologize, you may forgive me. If you do, you relieve any further obligation I have because you believe I am sincere in my apology and will repair my actions in the future. The moral scales are back in balance.

Our job as parents is to socialize our children and prepare them to face the world ahead of them. Our job as parents is to foster our children's development. We want our children to improve over time. When a child misbehaves, our job is to respond in a way that motivates a child to change her behavior for the better. If a child does something wrong, and we have done something to help him acknowledge his misbehavior and improve, what need is there for additional retribution? If we are genuinely able to get a child to see that his behavior has been wrong, then he is in the same position that I am in when I apologize sincerely and pledge to do better. If we are able to prompt children to appreciate their wrongdoings without resorting to punishment, then we have already balanced the moral scales. Further retribution is unnecessary to achieve the balance.

MOTIVATE COMPLIANCE

Clear and sensitive limit setting the first step in fostering moral development and harmonious family interactions.

=====

"Milk"
"Excuse me?"
"Milk"
"That's not how you ask. If you'd like me to pass the milk, you say, 'Would you pass the milk please?' Saying 'please' shows that you care that you are asking someone to do something for you."
"Would you pass the milk, please?"
"Yes, of course!"

This simple interaction contains almost everything a parent needs to know about how to motivate compliance in children. Mary wants some milk, but her mother wants her to use better manners. To motivate compliance, Mary's mother withholds the milk until her daughter asks for it in a polite way. Mary doesn't get what she wants until she complies with her mother's rules and requests.

In this chapter, we examine how parents can motivate compliance in children by managing the consequences of children's choice making. In most circumstances, redirecting children when they fail to meet our stated expectations is sufficient to motivate them to comply with rules and requests. However, this is not always the case. Children often resist parental directives, and when they do, parents need tools to enforce those rules and requests. A powerful way to motivate compliance in children is to control the circumstances under which children make choices that advance or fail to advance their interests.

We all make choices based on our interests. Our interests are simply the everyday wants, desires, and goals that motivate our behavior. In general, we find ourselves motivated in two different ways: we act either to get something that we want or to avoid something that we do not want. Given a choice, we all choose to behave in ways that we believe will advance our interests and avoid behaving in ways that we think will impede our interests. If this is so, then parents can motivate compliance in their children by structuring the circumstances of children's choice making. This can be accomplished in three basic ways:

- In disciplinary contexts, stop misbehavior from achieving its intended goal; teach children to develop alternative ways to advance their interests. When children misbehave, show them alternative ways to achieve their current goals in appropriate ways. For example, guide a boy through the process of getting a wanted toy by asking rather than grabbing.
- Hold children accountable for the consequences of misbehavior. For example, when a girl draws pictures on the wall, hold her responsible for cleaning up the mess.
- The option of enduring or avoiding the negative. When all else fails, motivate compliance by controlling the circumstances under which children can avoid unwanted outcomes. For example, if your daughter refuses to brush her teeth, she must sit silently until she chooses to comply. This strategy is the single most

effective way to motivate compliance in most situations.

Compliance Is Not a Four-Letter Word

Some parents—particularly those who endorse child-centered parenting practices—recoil from the idea that a child should be expected to comply with parental requests and directives. From a child-centered point of view, compliance is akin to obedience—a primary value of authoritarian parents. Studies show that that over the course of American and Western European history, there has been a steady decrease in the extent to which parents endorse values such as obedience in their children, and a corresponding increase in the extent to which they embrace values such as autonomy, self-expression, and initiative.[1] For some parents, to say that a child should comply with parental requests, directives, and rules casts the child in a passive role in relation to parents. The expectation of compliance might seem to undermine a child's budding autonomy and independence.

It is not unusual to hear parents cry out in frustration, "I wish my child would cooperate! He won't do anything I ask him to do!" This statement contains something of a contradiction. The term *cooperation* refers to the process of "operating together." Two people can cooperate if they are both more or less in control of their actions and can work together in pursuing some common goal. When a parent directs an unwilling child to pick up his toys, there is no common goal. The parent

---

1. Alwin, D. F. (1988). From obedience to autonomy: Changes in traits desired in children, 1924–1978. *Public Opinion Quarterly, 52*(1), 33–52.

Alwin, D., Beattie, B., Hannah, A., & Powell, E. (2011). Has Growth of the Egalitarian American Family Continued into the 21st Century. *Conference Papers—American Sociological Association,* 466.

Gullestad, M. (1996). From obedience to negotiation: Dilemmas in the transmission of values between generations in Norway. *Journal of the Royal Anthropological Institute, 2*(1), 25.

and the child want different things. As a result, the term *cooperate* is really being used as a euphemism for *comply*. The parent wants the child to adopt his agenda and do what is being asked of him. The parent who complains that her child "won't do anything I ask" is not looking for cooperation (except for the type of cooperation that can occur only after a child has accepted a parent's agenda); she is looking for compliance. She wants her child to honor her requests without a fuss.

Many contemporary American parents would seem to value self-expression, collaboration, and autonomy over compliance. They prefer the term *cooperate* over *comply* because the latter makes the child seem too subservient to the parent. The problem with this kind of thinking is that the route to cooperation and collaboration requires that children first gain the more basic capacity to comply with legitimate parental requests and limits. It is not possible to foster the development of autonomy, independence, or collaboration unless a child gains the capacity to regulate his impulses, emotions, and behavior and to respect the needs and wishes of others. At the most basic level, this involves getting children to comply with everyday rules, requests, and directives. In this way, compliance is the first step to the development of rule following, self-regulation, and moral understanding. After parents guide children through the acquisition of basic self-regulatory skills, they will be in a better position to engage children in the more cooperative, collaborative, and harmonious interactions they value so much.

Strategies for Motivating Compliance

The most effective ways to produce almost immediate compliance in children is to control the consequences of their choice making. If children act on the basis of their interests, they will be motivated to change their behavior if it is in their immediate interest to do so. This section contains three powerful ways to motivate compliance in children.

Teach Children Appropriate Ways
to Advance Their Interests

The first strategy for motivating compliance draws on children's natural, everyday interests. Children choose their actions based on their interests. Behind every action is a goal or interest—something a child wants. It is helpful to think of a child's interest as a kind of problem to be solved. The problem is how the child can get what she wants. Action is a kind of strategy that a child uses to try solving the problem. For example, Sam grabs a ball from Abbey because he wants to play with it. Grabbing the ball is one solution to Sam's problem of how to get the ball. If the grab is successful, he will have advanced his interests; he got what he wanted. If his grab comes up short, he will have failed to advance his goals. He didn't get what he wanted.

If a child's behavior is successful in bringing about his interest, it is likely that he will repeat the behavior in the future. If these strategies to advance his interests fail, he will be motivated to change his behavior to find new ways to reach his goals. Thus, if parents tolerate unwanted behavior, it is likely to be repeated. If parents are consistent in disrupting the success of an unwanted behavior, children will be less likely to continue to engage in the behavior. If Sam is allowed to succeed in his strategy of grabbing to get Abbey's ball, he will probably continue using this strategy in the future. If Sam's mother (or his sister herself) consistently takes the ball away from him when he grabs, his strategy will have failed. He will be less likely to use this strategy in the future.

It is not enough for parents simply to disrupt the success of a child's unwanted behavior. There is a reason Sam grabbed Abbey's ball—he wanted to play with it. Stopping Sam's grab from producing the result that he intended may discourage him from using grabbing as a way to get what he wants. It may also motivate Sam to find another way to advance his interests. However, children do not always know how to change their behavior in ways that will allow them to advance their interests or reach their goals! Alternatives to unacceptable behavior do not develop spontaneously. Children need to be taught successful alternatives to unwanted behavior. Refusing to tolerate unwanted behavior is a key to eliminating that behavior, but it does nothing to help the child find new, more appropriate, and more effective ways of acting.

Furthermore, merely telling children about alternative ways to behave is unlikely to be effective. Children—like anyone else—find it difficult to complete complex tasks using verbal instruction alone. (Trying to get one's sibling to share a toy is no easy task!) Instead, it is more helpful to demonstrate and even coach the child through the new behavior until the child reaches success. Coaching the child through to success is essential to ensure that he or she adopts the new behavior. In Sam's case, success would mean teaching Sam a strategy that might reasonably result in him being able to advance his interests (i.e., get a turn playing with the ball). He can be taught, for example, to ask Abbey for a turn with the ball. However, if Abbey refuses the request (a likely outcome given Sam's previous behavior), Sam's newfound skill would have failed to advance his interest.

There are a variety of alternative behaviors that Sam could be taught that could result in attaining his goal in an acceptable way. These include (but are not limited to) coaching Sam through the process of:

- asking a parent for a different desired toy, which the parent could provide.
- apologizing to Abbey, and then asking politely for a turn.
- proposing to play ball with Abbey.
- waiting patiently until Abbey was finished playing with her toy.

Task 4.1. Teaching Alternative Behaviors

Teaching alternatives to misbehaviors is a powerful way to motivate children while fostering closeness in the parent–child relationship. The key is to start with the interests that motivate your child's misbehavior. By acknowledging rather than repudiating these interests, a parent helps builds a trusting partnership with his or her child. Showing the child an alternative way to advance his interests motivates him to modify his behavior. For example, imagine an eight-year old child interrupts you when you are having a conversation with another adult. To teach an alternative to interrupting, the question for the parent becomes, "What is my child's interest?" The child wants to gain the parent's attention for a reason. At this point, having understood the child's motives, the task becomes one of blocking the intended outcome of the interruption and then showing the child a way that he can meet his interests successfully and appropriately. For example, a parent can tell the child to wait until there is a break in the conversation, and then say, "Mom, can I have your attention?" Ignoring any further interruptions by the child, the parent then gives the child her attention when the child shows the wanted behavior (waiting and then asking). The child learns that interrupting does not work to advance his interests, whereas waiting and asking politely does. Use the right side of the diagram to think of ways of teaching alternatives to misbehavior in your home.

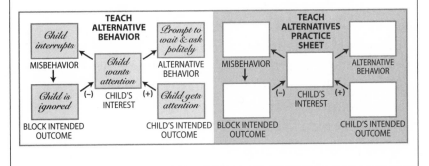

Hold Children Accountable for the Consequences of Their Actions

If Mary draws on the wall, she should be coached through the process of cleaning up the mess. If Terry carelessly loses his electronic game device, there are no guarantees that his parents will get a new one; he may have to save up to buy one himself. If Tim waits until the night before the concert to tell his mother he needs a new shirt, he may have to use an old one.

In punishment, the connection between the child's misbehavior and its punishing consequences is arbitrary. Mary drew pictures on the wall with her crayons. As a punishment, her father makes her go to bed early. The relationship between drawing on the wall and going to be early is arbitrary. Going to bed early has nothing to do with making pictures on the walls. Mary is likely to learn little or nothing about why she should not draw on the walls from being sent to bed early; it will teach nothing about the appropriate ways she can use her crayons to express herself.

Not all consequences are created equal. Mary drew on the wall. The most direct consequence of Mary's drawing on the wall was that it made a mess that has to be cleaned up.

Instead of being sent to bed, Mary can be required clean up the mess she made. By being required to wash the walls, Mary is being held responsible for the consequence of her actions. Unlike punishment, the connection between drawing on the wall and washing the wall is direct, not arbitrary. There are many connections Mary and her parent can make between making a mess on the wall and the act of having to wash it:

If I draw on the wall, it makes a mess.
If I draw on the wall, someone has to clean it.
If I draw on the wall, I will have to clean it.
If I draw on the wall, I will have to clean it—not Daddy.
It's hard to wipe crayons off of the wall.
When I have to clean the walls, I have to work very hard.

As is clear from this example, Mary's actions had consequences—not just for herself but also for other people. It is unlikely that she was thinking about the effect of her actions on other people when she was drawing on the wall. When she is required to take responsibility for her mess, she comes face to face with the effect of her actions on others. Cleaning up the mess says: "You did this. This is how it affects others. Now you have to take responsibility to repair the situation." This awareness is at the core of the development of responsibility and moral character.

Because of the relationship between the child's misbehavior and consequences of those behaviors, these types of consequences are sometimes called "natural consequences" or "logical consequences." However, to speak of such consequences as natural or logical can be misleading. There is nothing inherently natural about cleaning up one's mess, replacing a friend's toy that one has broken, or not having one's gadget replaced after having lost it. These are ethical consequences, not natural ones. Furthermore, many consequences may be considered natural but inappropriate as disciplinary strategies. No parent would allow his child to learn from the natural consequences of running into the street. The term *logical* does not provide greater clarity. It may be logical to clean up one's own mess; however, it is equally as logical to run away from the mess, hide it, or blame it on someone else! These may be logical reactions, not moral ones.

This is why it is better to refer to the types of consequences discussed here as meaningful consequences or, even better, as morally responsible consequences. We learn what we do, and particularly what we do with others. If a child misbehaves and is required to take responsibility for the consequences of that misbehavior, he learns to do more than simply associate that behavior with some unpleasant experience. The child learns to identify the consequences of his actions, become aware the effects they have on self and others, and develop a sense of moral standards that he can use to guide his behavior in future situations.

Task 4.2. Delivering Meaningful Consequences

Like teaching alternative behaviors, the key to arranging meaningful consequences for children's misbehaviors is to focus on children's interests. The relation between the consequence of a child's actions and the interests that motivate those actions is what makes the consequence meaningful. As shown in the left side of the diagram, when a child commits a misdeed, the parent asks, "What is my child's interest? What motivates the behavior?" For example, a young girl colors on the wall to make pretty pictures, to exercise the joy of coloring, or even perhaps to make a prize for her parents! A meaningful consequence to this action not only disrupts the child's intended outcome but also forces her to accept responsibility for her actions (e.g., cleaning up the mess). You can use the left side of the diagram to think of ways to arrange meaningful consequences to typical misbehaviors that occur in your home.

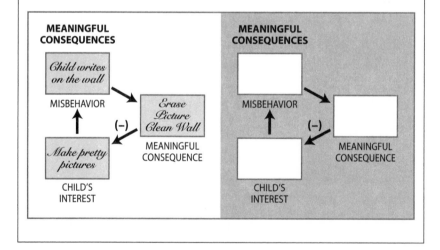

When All Else Fails: Motivate Children to Remove the Unwanted

Recall that there are two basic way of being motivated in the world: we can act to produce something wanted or to avoid something unwanted. The motivation to avoid something unwanted is powerful. It occurs quite often, even though we may not always be aware of it. We open the window when it is too hot; loosen our shoelaces when they are too tight; take a pain reliever when we have a headache. All of these are examples of occasions that we perform some action (open the window, loosen the shoe, taking a pain reliever) to remove something that we don't want (a hot room, a tight shoe, a headache).

Drawing on the natural inclination to remove unwanted outcomes is an extremely effective way to motivate compliance in children. Here are three simple examples.

Five-year-old Frances and her mother are at the supermarket. They are about to leave the store. Frances complains that she is tired and can't walk by herself. Her mother tells her that she is a big girl and can walk. Frances sits down on the sidewalk. At this point, Frances's mother says, "I'm leaving now!" and walks down the sidewalk. Frances jumps up and runs to her mother's side. She takes her mother's hand and they walk to the car.

Seven-year-old Charlie is fussing at the table. He is anxious to leave the table to watch a television program. Not wanting to finish his meal, he plays with his food and states that he is full. His mother insists that he finish his meal. Charlie refuses. His mother says, "I know you that you want to go and watch TV. However, I want you to finish your food. You have a choice. You can sit in the chair quietly with nothing to do, or you can finish your meal. You aren't getting up until you are through." Charlie refused and asked his mother to let him go. After his mother ignored his requests, Charlie quickly gobbled up his food and went to watch TV.

Ten-year-old Jack's father asked him to clean his room. Over the course of the day, Jack played computer games, listened to music, and did some reading. It was almost time for him to go over to a friend's house for a sleepover. His father reminded him that he needed to clean his room. Jack complained, saying that he didn't have the time to do it before he left. Jack's father said, "There will be no sleepover until your room is cleaned." Reluctantly, Jack cleaned his room.

In each situation, a child refused to comply with a request made by the parent. Each involves a situation in which the child is asked to engage in some action that was unwanted by the child. Using this procedure, the child is placed in a situation in whey they have the opportunity to remove themselves from an unwanted situation by complying with the parent's request. In essence, the child elects to either remove himself from an unwanted situation by complying with the parent's request or remain in the unwanted situation but continue to refuse the parent's request.

In the context of noncompliance, parents often resort to a variety of ineffective disciplinary techniques. These include threatening punishment ("If you don't finish your meal you are going to bed early"), punishing ("You've lost your computer privileges for a week"), bribing ("If you finish your meal, you can stay up 15 minutes later"), and offering rewards (praising the child for taking a bite of food). In each of these strategies, the child has the opportunity to refuse to comply with the parent's directive. The likelihood that children will comply with parental directives is much higher using when "removing the negative" than it is with any of these disciplinary techniques. This is because in these other techniques, the child retains the ability to refuse to comply with the parent's directive. The child can simply ignore the threat, accept the punishment, refuse the bribe, or ignore the offered rewards. In contrast, when removing the negative, although it is possible for a child to choose to continue to refuse the parent's request, such a choice is unlikely because doing so is inconsistent with the child's desire to remove himself from an unwanted situation.[2]

The "remove the negative" procedure is particularly effective in helping parents gain or regain the capacity to regulate noncompliant children. There are many reasons children may become noncompliant in their relationships with parents. A common problem is simply the failure to place clear limitations on children's behavior and enforce compliance. This problem arises quite often in families in which parents use permissive or child-centered parenting strategies. Happily, in the vast majority of such circumstances, by sensitively applying consistent limits on children's behavior, parents can foster the development of compliance in their children.

Many parents find the initial process of enforcing compliance in their children to be emotionally difficult. For many parents, being a loving parent means wanting to make children experience positive feelings and protecting them from negative ones. Parents naturally feel sympathy and empathy for their children. Some parents experience feelings of guilt when they feel as though they have caused their children to experience negative feelings during disciplinary encounters. These are common feelings. They are often exacerbated in parents who are working to make the transition from more permissive or child-centered parenting practices to a more authoritative approach. Children who are not accustomed to having limits

---

2. Some might object that the "choice" given to the child in the remove the negative procedure is not genuine. Instead, it is an illusory choice between two negatives over which the parent has ultimate control. However, this objection has merit only under the child-centered belief that children should be afforded the freedom not to comply with legitimate parental directives. The parent–child relationship is not one between equals. Parents have the right and the responsibility to determine the limits of children's choice making. For an authoritative parent, the question of whether the child can be afforded a genuinely free choice is one that has already been settled by the very terms of the parent–child relationship. The child's choice is never fully "free"; it is necessarily constrained by the parent's responsibility to make determinations about the well-being of the child.

placed on them have often developed sophisticated skill for negotiating their way out of complying with parental requests. When their parents begin to place limits on them, both the child and parent are often unprepared for the level of emotional upset that can ensue.

The experience of negative emotions in children is a necessary and inevitable part of the developmental process. It plays an important role in disciplinary encounters. A certain degree of emotional arousal is necessary to attend to and benefit from disciplinary encounters. Furthermore, the practice of protecting children from experiencing negative emotions can prevent them from developing the capacity to cope with emotionally difficult situations. These skills are essential for the normative emotional development of children.

The initial difficulty that some parents have when dealing with negative emotions in their children is illuminated in the following example of a father learning to discipline his three-year-old daughter.

> *Nava is a three-year-old girl. Her parents complained that she would not come when called and that she routinely refused to do what was asked of her. Under the guidance of a parenting coach, it was decided that the family would focus on the skill of getting Nava to come to dinner when called. One evening, on being called to dinner, Nava continued to play as usual. Under the coach's instruction, her father picked her up and sat her on the floor in a hallway connecting the living room to the kitchen. Her father said, "You can get up when you are ready to come to dinner." The father was asked to be present, but not talk further with the girl. Nava immediately ran back to her toys. Without speaking, the father repeated his previous action. As the girl began to run away again, the father, unsure about how to proceed, asked for assistance. The coach suggested that the father simply hold his hands out to prevent the girl from running. Although hesitant, the father perse-*

vered. Over the next several minutes, Nava became increasingly emotional. She cried, screamed, and whimpered—essentially throwing a temper tantrum. The father, a compassionate and empathetic individual, found it difficult to continue the routine and at several points doubted his ability to do so. Nonetheless, after several minutes, Nava calmed down. After a brief reparation period in which the father and child hugged and talked affectionately, the girl was able to come to dinner.

This is not an atypical experience for parents who, experiencing the frustration of living with a dysregulated or noncompliant child, summon the courage to work toward more authoritative child management strategies. Over time, with persistent effort, children begin to become more regulated, calm, compliant, and cooperative. As this occurs, the emotional climate of the family can begin to shift. Interactions previously filled with conflict begin to operate more smoothly and with less emotional disruption. After experiencing transformations like these, many parents find that their families have moved closer to the harmonious ideals they had originally sought to cultivate using more child-centered strategies.

Task 4.3. Getting Out of Jail

It can be difficult to understand the remove the negative technique. The difficulty is often removed once we think of a child's motivation to remove the negative as a form of escape. Motivating children to remove the negative is like putting a child in jail and then explaining what he has to do to get out. Think of removing the negative as getting out of jail. When all else fails, find that thing that your child hates the most of all—your child's version of "jail." It might be sitting by himself, not being able to go to the party on Friday night, not being able to play with his friends, and so on. Then, put your child in that jail until he performs the wanted behavior. You can say, "I see you have not cleaned your room despite my having asked you many times. You are now done playing; instead of playing you must sit in this chair and do nothing" (assuming that this is your child's version of jail). "You cannot get off the chair until you choose to [i.e., get out of jail] clean your room. Once you clean your room, you will be out of jail and free to play again." See the text to understand how this technique is different from punishment. Use the right portion of the diagram to identify ways you can motivate wanted behavior by offering your child the chance to get out of jail.

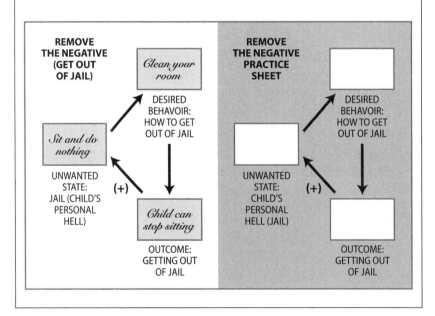

Earning by Learning: A Variant of the Remove the Negative Procedure

The earning by learning strategy is based on the idea that disciplinary situations can be treated as teaching and learning moments. Disciplinary situations can be seen as opportunities for teaching and learning new skills. When children fail to conform to expectations, there is usually a reason for it. Some of the reasons have to do with motivation—children may not want to comply for some reason. Susan refuses to finish her dinner because she doesn't like the taste of her vegetables. Ted doesn't clean his room because he would rather play outside. Molly lies because she is afraid of getting into trouble. In other situations, children may lack the skills (or some part of the skills) to conform to some expectation. Susan interrupts because she hasn't yet mastered the skill of waiting her turn to speak. Luis doesn't clean his room because he is overwhelmed by the task. Jack goes over his allotted time on the computer because he hasn't mastered the skill of monitoring his time properly.

Regardless of whether a misbehavior has its origins in lack of motivation or in a skill that has not yet been fully acquired, it is possible to think of discipline as an opportunity to teach a child what she needs to do to follow a rule. Imagine that Ted avoids cleaning his room because he is overwhelmed by the task. He starts to clean his room; however, because he finds it difficult, he quickly becomes distracted. He needs help in two areas: learning to break down the task of cleaning his room and sustaining his motivation to complete this difficult task.

In the earning by learning technique, the child who has consistently broken a rule is given the opportunity to earn back a desired privilege by building the skills needed to follow the rule or directive. The logic of this technique goes like this: Ted avoids the task of cleaning his room. Even though cleaning his room is within range of his developing abilities, Ted needs a push to motivate him to invest the time and effort required to master the skill and put it into practice. To use the earning by learning procedure:

1. As a consequence of the child's misbehavior, take away a privilege or activity that the child desires—optimally one that is related to the child's misbehavior.
2. Give the child the opportunity to earn back the privilege by learning how to conform to the rule that the child has broken.
3. Teach the child what he has to do to follow the rule that has been broken.
4. Find a way to monitor the child's progress through to mastery. When the child has mastered the skill, the parent restores the previously revoked privilege.

Here is how one family put the earning by learning technique into practice.

Nine-year-old Marty was getting difficult to deal with. He seemed to think he was the center of the universe. He didn't say "Please" or "Thank you." He didn't seem grateful for anything. He walked around thinking that somehow the world owed him whatever he wanted. He was an entitled little boy. His mother and father grew tired of Marty's bad attitude. To implement the earning by learning technique, Marty's parents asked themselves: What does Marty love most of all? What does he feel he is most entitled to? Computer time. Marty's parents decided to teach him that computer time is a privilege and not a given. Marty's mother said: "You are walking around here thinking that you are entitled to anything you want! You whine when you don't get what you want! You don't seem grateful for what you have. We're tired of this type of behavior. You get one hour of computer time per day. Having a computer is a privilege. It's not something you are owed. Feeling grateful means being aware that you couldn't have the computer at all if it were not for other people—in this case, you couldn't have the computer without kindness of your father and me."

Marty's parents revoked his computer privileges. To earn the privileges back, over the next several days or weeks— however long it took—Marty was required to identify 20 times that he benefited from the kind actions of someone else in some way. On each occasion, he was required to thank the person and record the incident on a card that his parents made for him. The card simply contained 20 slots on which Marty could describe what happened. He was highly motivated. He wasted no time identifying his 20 grateful moments. He completed the task over a series of several days. When he proudly showed his completed card to his father, Marty's computer privileges were restored.

In implementing the earning by learning strategy, Marty was able to earn by a desired privilege by learning a skill related to that privilege. In so doing, Marty's parents were able to use their son's deep interests to motivate him to work toward the development of a general skill, namely, expressing (and perhaps even feeling) gratitude. By the time earning by learning process was over, Marty demonstrated that he was able to recognize situations in which he was the beneficiary of someone's kindness and express gratitude for their kind act. After the earning by learning experience, Marty spontaneously expressed gratitude more often. However, his parents still had to remind him to do so on many occasions. New skills take time to develop. Although Marty improved, his progress was only a single step in a longer process of cultivating gratitude.

Frequently Asked Questions

How Does Removing the Negative Differ from Punishment?

The remove the negative procedure is extremely powerful in motivating children to learn new skills while also learning to

comply with parental rules, expectations, and directives. Its
effectiveness comes from the natural power our desire to
remove ourselves from unpleasant situations. Recall that children and adults alike can be motivated in two ways: to obtain
something wanted or to avoid something unwanted. The
remove the negative technique draws on the second type of
situation. In this procedure, the child is not simply motivated
to avoid something that may happen in the future, she is motivated to remove something unpleasant that is going on right
now—and will continue to go on until the child does something to stop it. This is a strong stuff, because the unpleasant
situation does not go away; it sits there demanding the child's
attention until the child does something about it.

This is also the key to understanding how removing the negative differs from punishment. They seem to be the same
because both involve something unpleasant or negative. Punishment is by definition something that is unpleasant. A child
is punished for not finishing her dinner by being required to sit
quietly in the chair for some period. Removing the negative
also involves something unpleasant. A child who refuses to finish her dinner is required to sit quietly until she complies.
These situations involve the same misbehavior (refusing to finish dinner), the same desired behavior (finishing dinner), and
the same basic consequence (sitting alone quietly). However,
what differs is the way the consequence and the desired behavior are related. Let's explore how.

In punishment, a child is placed in an unpleasant situation
as a consequence for some misbehavior. The child is expected
to associate the unpleasant consequence (sitting alone quietly)
with the unwanted behavior (refusing to finish dinner). In the
remove the negative procedure, the child is not simply given
an unpleasant consequence; the child is given an unpleasant
consequence that can be removed only by complying with the
parental directive. In the remove the negative procedure, the
child must actually produce the desired behavior (finishing
dinner) as a precondition for being allowed to remove himself

from the unpleasant situation. As a result, the child is all but compelled to comply with the parent's directive to escape from an unwanted and continuously ongoing situation. This differs from punishment because punishment, even though it involves a negative consequence, nonetheless gives the child the freedom not to comply with the parent's directive.

To remove the negative procedure puts conditions on the child that punishment does not. When removing the negative, the child must actually produce the behavior desired by the parent in the disciplinary context. As a result, the child (1) learns to tolerate the emotional difficulty of performing the task; (2) experiences the feelings associated with success in performing the act (e.g., relief in getting it over with, surprise that it may not have been as anticipated, pride over accomplishment); and, perhaps most important, (3) learns that noncompliance will not be tolerated. As a result, children are more likely to carry the behavior forward into similar situations in the future.

Punishment is based on the idea that as the child comes to associate her misdeed with some unpleasant consequence, she will refrain from performing the unwanted behavior in the future. The problem is that the punishing consequence is only tangentially related (if at all) to the conditions necessary to foster the development of desired behavior. At best, when punished, the child learns that in the future, if she engages in certain behaviors, she is likely to receive an unpleasant consequence. However, the connection between the unpleasant consequence (sitting quietly alone) and the misdeed (refusing to finish dinner) is simply too remote to function as an effective disciplinary strategy.

What about Time Outs?

Time outs are rarely if ever used for the purpose that they were intended. Time outs were never intended to be used as a form of punishment. However, in practice, they are almost always used that way. The concept of time out is based on the idea that if we are engaged in some form of sustained activity, we must be getting something out of it. Children act to advance their interests; if a child's actions are working for him, then he must be getting something from it. The time-out procedure provides a strategy to break the connection between a child's ongoing behavior and the positive consequences that may be assumed to follow the behavior.

For example, Jerrie repeatedly hits Joey when they are playing together. Jerrie may be getting something positive out of hitting Joey. She may be successfully trying to annoy him, trying to retaliate for some infraction, trying to get Joey to do something, and so on. The appropriate use of the time-out procedure would simply involve asking Jerrie to remove herself from the situation and take a break. The parent might also suggest that she try to calm herself or reflect on the situation. The logic of the procedure is that removing Jerrie from the situation breaks the link between her action (hitting) and whatever positive consequence she experienced from her hitting. The time out is meant to provide time away from the positive consequences of a child's unwanted actions. The process of constructive parenting begins after the break. At this point, the parent and child could reflect on the problem together, engage in a problem-solving discussion, and so forth.

Carried out in this way, the time-out procedure is meant to provide an alternative to punitive parenting practices. Although it was intended to provide a nonpunitive way to respond to children's misbehavior, currently it is most typically used as a form of punishment. It is not usual to hear a parent say, "If you keep doing that, you're going to get a time out." When this happens, the parent has transformed what was initially meant to be a quiet break into a negative consequence for misbehavior. This is the essence of punishment.

When used as a punishment, the time-out procedure often backfires. The ineffective use of time out can lead to the escalation of unwanted behavior, rather than its termination. Not surprisingly, children who are given time outs often resist their use. This is especially true of children who are given time outs for behavior problems, such as acting out or talking back. Following is an example of how the time-out procedure as a punishment produced escalation of problem behavior between a staff member and a child in a group home.

> It was the end of the "quiet time." Having finishing an activity, Tom, with a pencil in hand, walked toward two boys, jumped over a game board, and sat on the couch waiting to be dismissed to his room. A staff member yelled to him, "Time out!" Tom asked, "Why?" The staff member replied, "You know why!" Tom began to argue with her. The staff member replied, "You just got yourself ten, mister." Tom began his time out and began to cry. The staff member informed him he was at his "warning"—a level of escalation beyond which Tom would have to be taken to the crisis room. At this point, the boy used a profanity toward the staff member and was taken away.

When used appropriately and for its intended purpose, the time-out procedure can be effective in putting a stop to misbehavior and initiating a process of calming and deescalation. Used ineffectively or as a punishment, the time-out procedure runs all of the risk of other forms of punishment.

Is Spanking Harmful?

The question of spanking is controversial in both public and scientific circles. Spanking and all forms of corporal punishment are, of course, types of punishment. As argued here, punishment is ineffective as a long-term disciplinary strategy. It reduces unwanted behavior only in the short run when the threat of punishment is looming, or in the long run when the punishment is very severe. As elaborated in this book, there are many other effective forms of discipline. As a form of punishment, spanking is no exception to this rule. It is neither necessary nor productive to spank a child.

Nonetheless, the question remains controversial. Punishment has long been a popular disciplinary method, and spanking is the quintessential punishment. Many parents continue to spank their children. Given this reality, one might ask, "Is spanking harmful?" It depends on what one means by "spanking," and what one means by "harm."

Research is unambiguously clear that severe physical punishment is detrimental to children's development. Severe physical punishment involves the intentional attempt to inflict injury or physical harm onto a child. It is often accompanied by emotionally hurtful words that can be extremely damaging to a child's developing sense of self and capacity to relate to others. Severe physical punishment is associated with increases in what are called internalizing (depression, fearfulness, anxiety) and externalizing (acting out, aggression, rule violation) behavior in children. Such forms of punishment are considered to be forms of child abuse and are illegal in every state in the United States. There is no ambiguity about the damaging effects of harsh forms of punitive discipline.

The research on the harmful effects of less severe forms of physical punishment (spanking) is less clear. Light spanking refers to the use of the hand to administer a relatively low level of discomfort to a child. Is "light spanking" harmful to children? It is difficult to draw simple conclusions from available research. Many studies suggest that light spanking is associated with higher levels of behavior problems in children. Other studies show minimal associations or none at all. When researchers do find such associations, it is often difficult to know whether spanking is the cause. For example, does spanking children cause them to act out more often? Or are children who show disposition to act out more difficult to handle, and thus cause frustrated parents to choose spanking as a disciplinary strategy?

The most likely interpretation of the available evidence is that in the specific case of occasional light spankings (e.g., a slap on the hand, a spank to the buttocks), especially when they delivered by parents who are otherwise supportive, warm, and communicative, are probably not harmful to any great degree or in any clearly discernible way. However, such a limited and tepid conclusion is hardly an endorsement for the use of spanking as a disciplinary strategy. In most circumstances, physical punishment is associated with increased levels of behavior problems. There are much better and more effective forms of discipline.

FOSTER EMOTIONAL DEVELOPMENT

Lead carefully by leading with care.

An infant's first encounters with the world are social and emotional ones. Infants are most alive when they are engaged in emotionally charged face-to-face interactions with their caregivers. From the earliest ages, babies enter in social interaction as partners in richly animated dances with their caregivers. The infant sees his mother; he smiles and coos. His mother smiles back and imitates her child's cooing. The pair exchanges smiles and coos until the infant begins to lose interest or become overstimulated. At this point, a sensitive parent backs off and may begin to approach her child with more soothing than exciting tones. All subsequent development is built on the foundation of these richly social and emotional interactions.

Emotions do not become less important as time goes on. Social relationships rely on a child's capacity to feel appreciated and secure in her social interactions with others. Psychologists have demonstrated that "emotional intelligence"—the capacity to understand and act on one's sense of the emotional life of others—is at least as important as intellectual ability in building a happy and successful life. Furthermore, the task of cultivating a meaningful and happy life is not born of cold thought. Happy people adopt a particular social and emotional orientation toward life—one that embraces the virtues of gratitude, compassion, moderation, and love.

Authoritative parents lead with care. This means at least two things. First, when authoritative parents lead, they do so carefully. When they direct their children, they are careful to take their children's interests and feelings into consideration. As a result, as they lead, authoritative parents teach their children how to direct their own thinking, feeling, and acting. Through such sensitive direction parents support the development of children's emotional autonomy. A second way authoritative parents lead with care is by putting care first. This means acting out of love—that is, acting out of a desire to continuously care for and nurture the child and his development. With care children develop a deep sense of being appreciated in the world. Thus, through their emotional interactions with caregivers, children develop a sense of themselves as both appreciated and self-directed and carry these emotional dispositions forward into their later projects and social relationships.

What Emotions Are and Why They're Important

An emotion is a reaction to the fate of our concerns. Behind every emotion is some type of interest—a want, goal, desire, or concern. Something has happened to something that we want. For example, we are sad when we experience a loss of something we wanted and we can't get it back; behind every sadness is the loss of something valued. We are afraid when we sense danger; in fear, we are concerned about being harmed. We are angry when things aren't the way they are supposed to be; in anger, we are concerned with something that has gone wrong. We feel guilty when we are responsible for some wrongdoing; when we feel guilt, we are motivated to avoid being a bad person. We are embarrassed when we seem like a fool in the eyes of others. We feel shame when we look at ourselves through the eyes of others and realize that we are a bad or horrible person; in shame, we are concerned with who we are in the eyes of others.

When we experience an emotion, something has happened that has affected our wants, goals, standards, and concerns. As a result, we experience a particular type of feeling. We reveal the feeling by the way we express it our face, voice, and body. For example, in anger, our eyebrows tend to furrow; we often tend to show our teeth, we raise our voice; our body becomes tense, and so on. This all happens automatically—we aren't aware of it.

Emotions are there for a reason. They have many functions. When we experience an emotion, the feeling part of the emotion alerts us that something important has happened. It makes us feel the importance of the event. When we feel anger, for example, the feeling alerts us that something is not the way it should be. It says, "Look, something is wrong—attend to it!" Emotions do this even before we are aware of what is happening. That is why we sometimes have a feeling about something before we can figure out why we have the feeling.

Our inner feelings are there to help us become aware of important situations. In contrast, outer expressions are there to make other people aware of our feelings. This is how parents come to know that their children are in need. When a parent witnesses a child wince, cry, and rub his arm, she knows that child is in pain. When a child averts her gaze and blushes when you ask if she stole the cookies, you know that she is feeling guilty. A child's emotional expression is a window into her internal world. This expression not only reveals how she feels, it reveals the type of thing that has happened to make her feel that way. With this information, parents can begin to attend to children in ways that are sensitive to their needs.

Tending Responsively to Children's Emotions

Emotions are fundamental. To be attuned with your child's emotions is to be sensitive to what is happening to her needs, goals, desires, and wants. Let's examine what it means be responsive to a child's emotions.

> *Six-year-old Jan and her father were picking strawberries. Jan's father was walking her through the strawberry fields and helping her approach some of the plants. Just as Jan was about to pick a berry, a black cat poked his face from beneath the leaves of the plant. Jan's body stiffened. As her eyes widened, her cheeks and eyebrows rose upward; her mouth opened. As her face held all these signs of fear, she looked at her father with a half-smile, as if to say, "I know I shouldn't be afraid but I am." Looking alternatively at Jan and the cat, her father said in a soft and comforting, "It's just a kitty; it won't hurt you." Jan turned her body away from the cat and ran toward her father. She turned again to look at the cat, and her face became serious as she watched the animal move slowly in her direction. Jan clung to her father's side and, hiding slightly behind him, kept his body between her and the cat.*

What's going on here? This is an everyday interaction. Though simple, it reveals a great deal about Jan, her relationship with her father, and her emotions. Jan is afraid of the cat. Her feelings, however, are complex. When she initially saw the cat, she stiffened in fear. Through her fear, however, she was able to look at her father and produce a half-smile. Her smile seemed to suggest both a plea for help as well as a sense that she knew she was not really in danger. Her father's soothing message seemed to give Jan just enough courage to break her "freeze" reaction and flee to his protection.

At this point, Jan's father is at a choice point—what should he do? He doesn't want her to be afraid. If he removes Jan (or the cat) from the situation, he can assuage his daughter's fear. If he encourages Jan to approach the cat, perhaps she can conquer her fear. What should he do? The answer depends on the intensity of Jan's emotions and her father's sense of whether learning to approach the cat is within Jan's learning zone. In the situation described here, Jan seems to feel protected by her father; she does not seem overwhelmed by her fear (which would require a different approach altogether). In this case, her father chose to introduce her slowly to the cat.

> *Jan's father crouched down between Jan and the cat, keeping his body between the two. He reached out and, petting the cat, said, "What a nice kitty." Looking back at Jan and still petting the cat, he said, "See? She's not going to hurt you." After a short period, he moved his body back slightly to open some space between Jan and the cat. "Wanna pet her?" Jan shook her head no and remained staring transfixed on the cat. Her father said, "Go ahead, just give her a little pet . . . just touch her." Jan hesitated, then slowly reached forward, touched the cat quickly, and immediately moved away.*

In this situation, Jan's father relies on his daughter's emotions to make decisions about how best to guide her. What has happened as a result of this simple interaction?

1. Jan has learned that her father is emotionally available to her when she is feeling anxious, afraid, or emotionally challenged in some way.
2. Jan has learned that her father is concerned about her; she feels protected and cared for.
3. Jan has learned how to approach the cat and even touch it despite her fear. She has learned that she can touch the cat without being hurt.
4. Jan's father has helped moderate the intensity of Jan's emotions. This is how children learn to regulate their emotions. Over time, Jan will gain the ability to regulate her own emotions in ways that are similar to how her father helped calm her. She may say to her-

self, "It's a nice kitty; it's not going to hurt me," or,
more important, "I pet the kitty before, I can do it
again."

5. Jan has begun to develop a sense of being confident
in approaching the cat. She has learned that she can
begin to overcome her fear by persevering. In situations that are similar to this one, she will feel more
secure in her ability to move beyond her comfort
zone.

As children grow older, this type of exchange between them
and their parents will occur many times in different forms. A
younger child may seek the emotional reassurance of her
mother when she is visiting the home of a friend; feeling secure,
she can enjoy success in playing with new toys and meeting
new people. An older child, aware that his parents are emotionally available, may seek assistance when his homework becomes
difficult, or when he is having difficulty with a friend or with a
teacher at school. Being responsive to children's emotions and
needs helps children learn to trust that parents will be "there"
for them. This provides the emotional foundation of a secure
and responsive parent–child relationship. It is within such
trusting and guiding relationships that children learn to be
competent in the world. Children are not naturally autonomous; they learn to control their actions and emotions through
their relationships with others.

The Three Bears of Emotion Management: Getting it Just Right

In the situation just described, Jan was afraid of a new and
unfamiliar cat. Her father became aware of her fear and was
able to respond sensitively. This is what it means to be emotionally responsive. However, in being responsive to Jan's fear,
Jan's father did not eliminate Jan's discomfort. Instead, he mod-

ulated her emotions and helped her keep them at a level that was optimal for learning. As describe, our emotions are there for a reason. Our goal as parents should not be to reduce the intensity of a child's emotions to zero. A certain degree of engagement and emotional arousal is necessary for effective learning to take place. If social relationships are built on emotion, we do not want to eliminate children's emotions. Instead, we should always seek to bring them into an optimal range of functioning.

We all know what Goldilocks was looking for as she sampled the three bowls of porridge: not too hot, not too cold, but just right. Like anything, when helping our children adjust to emotional situations, getting it "just right" is easier said than done. Happily, however, we don't have to get it just right all the time. Instead, we simply need to get it just right most of the time. Even better, giving just the right emotional guidance is more a matter getting to the right range than finding any single fixed point. Let's examine another situation.

> *Eight-year-old Carmen is doing her math homework. It's hard. In frustration, she repeats, "I can't do it! This is stupid! I can't do it." She throws her pencil down. "I'm never gonna be able to do this! Why do I need to know this?"*

Carmen is in a vulnerable state. Her developing sense of self is at stake. How do we respond to her? We want to avoid the extremes of pushing too much or not pushing enough. We want to get it just right. But how do we know what's just right? This can be very difficult. A good place to start is with your child's emotions. If we want children to be able to manage their own emotions, we have to start by modulating and managing their emotions for them. Gradually, as they become more emotionally competent, we turn the task of emotional management over to the children themselves.

Supporting Children through Moderate Levels of Challenge

Like all of us, children cannot learn well under conditions of intense, strong, or overwhelming emotion. The opposite is also true—children cannot learn if they not emotionally aroused *enough*. Children learn best—including learning how to cope with their own emotions—under in contexts in which adults provide and support children through moderate levels of challenge.

This idea is shown in Figure 5.1, which shows what happens to children's capacity to learn under conditions of increasing levels of emotional challenge. As shown in the figure, if the level of challenge provided to a child is too high, they will experience a range of negative emotions, such as frustration, anger, sadness, embarrassment, and shame. If the child's emotion is genuine, this is a signal to reduce the level of challenge and stimulation.

Under such circumstances, it is not be helpful to reduce the level of challenge to zero! To learn, children must be emotion-

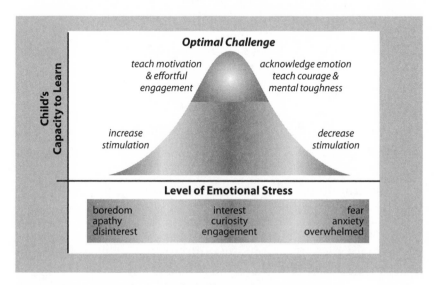

Figure 5.1. Optimal Level of Challenge for Learning

ally aroused and engaged. If we reduce the level of challenge and stimulation too much, the child will become bored, apathetic, disinterested, or perhaps even disrespectful or nonchalant! This is not a formula for learning or for emotional development. If the child's emotional engagement in a task is too low, it may becomes necessary to increase the challenge and level of stimulation given to the child.

The key is to find a moderate level of challenge and stimulation—not too much, not too little, but just right for the task at hand. When children are provided with moderate challenge, they become more alert, engaged, interested, and curious. When you are able to consistently provide children with moderate levels of challenge, they learn that you will be sensitive to their emotional needs. However, they will also learn that you mean business: when something is difficult, we don't just crawl in a corner and pout. We face it—initially with support, and thereafter increasingly on our own—in an attempt to learn from the situation.

Teaching Emotional Management through Moderate Challenge

If Carmen is experiencing difficulty with her math, she will be frustrated, angry, and perhaps demoralized. In this situation, she is not going to be able to learn. Again, the goal of the adult in such a situation is to modulate the level of challenge to make it more intellectually and emotionally manageable for the child.

Once Carmen's emotions have been brought to a more manageable state, it is time to start teaching—not just math but also emotional management. We learn what we do—not simply what we are told—and particularly what we do under the guidance of others. Thus, when you break down the math problem for the child, hold the child to attainable standards of perseverance, manage the child's frustration en route to success, and so on, you are teaching not only the practical skill in question (math) but also the essential skill of managing emotions.

If the child's level of motivation and emotional engagement begin to wane, the adult has to make a judgment. Is the child getting too tired? If so, it may be time to stop and revisit the issue later. If not, it may be time to provide guidance and instruction on the need to increase one's level of alertness, attention, and effort in the task. Is the child getting overwhelmed? If so, perhaps it's time to take a break. What if the adult makes the judgment that the child is capable of more, but simply has not built skills to manage frustration or difficult emotion? If that is so, it might be necessary to set the bar a bit higher. An adult might choose to offer guidance and instruction about the need for mental toughness or even courage in the process of working through difficult tasks. After all, to encourage is to foster courage as one deals with difficult tasks and events.

It is not always easy to make judgments about a child's emotional capacity. Such judgments are more art than science and are heavily dependent on how well an adult knows a child, their relationship history, and the adult's values. What's more, a child's capacity to manage emotion in difficult situations not only changes as he or she develops but will be different in different tasks and situations, even at different times of the day! We do not have to get it right every time. As long as we make consistent, good-faith efforts to strike the delicate balance between emotional nurturance and emotional challenge, we almost cannot help but get it just right more often than not.

Fostering Autonomy in Children

Children—like all people—have a need to affect their world. We want to make things happen. By the age of two, children are able to verbalize their desire to "do it myself!" Contemporary parents tend to place high value the development of autonomy in their children. We use the term *autonomy* to refer to the ability to be self-determining, to make decisions for oneself, to carry out tasks and responsibilities independently, to forge a path free from coercion. The capacity to be able to exert control over one's life is foundational to a child's emotional development. However, the concept of autonomy is tricky. We tend to think of autonomy as a virtue—something that is morally good. Aristotle warned us that virtues can easily turn into vices when they are taken to the extreme. As a result, there are two ways that autonomy can go wrong—we can have either too little of it or too much of it. In contemporary American culture, when we err, we do so on the side of granting children too much autonomy too early in development.

Parents sometimes err on the side of too much autonomy because they believe that children learn best when learning comes from within. From this view, children learn best when they are able to direct their own actions and make their own choices. As a result, the role of parents is not so much to lead but to follow the child's lead; the concern is that too much direction can promote conformity over autonomy. However, to be autonomous is to be able to do something—tell the time, choose a friend, decide what to have for lunch—on one's own. No child is born able to do such things, let alone carry them out alone. To perform a task autonomously is to have the knowledge and skill to carry it out appropriately and responsibly. Children do not gain the capacity to do so without the slow, sensitive guidance of other people. It follows that autonomy is something to be granted slowly over time, rather than something that should be simply bestowed.

Tending to Children's Autonomy Needs

Supporting the development of a child's sense of autonomy is an essential part of a child's emotional development. As already indicated, from the earliest ages, children seek to gain some degree of control over their worlds. However, children's capacity for autonomy in any given area of life is limited. Granting children autonomy before they are able to master the skills necessary to make those choices increases the likelihood of failure, poor performance, frustration, and self-doubt. There are several ways to support a child's need for autonomy in any given context.

First, whenever possible and appropriate, seek to involve a child in shared activities and decision making at the level that is appropriate for the child's development. Just because a child wants to be able to make his own decisions doesn't mean he is ready or able to do so. However, children are able to be active participants in many activities that affect them. The trick is to make room for the children to participate in shared activities and decision making in ways that are sensitive to their developmental levels and the parent's rules and interests.

> "You can have vegetable soup or a tuna sandwich—you choose!"
>
> "If you want to help mommy, take this brush and paint this part of the wall here. Don't go outside of the lines I've painted for you. And stay on the newspapers."
>
> "We are going to have movie night. But we all have to agree on a movie to watch. We want to hear what movies you want to watch, but you can't just say 'no' to everyone else's choices."

Second, whenever possible, identify with the child's interests and projects. Over the course of child rearing, children will inevitably come into conflict with a parent's rules, interests, and standards. As a result, it is easy for children to come to feel that they are at odds with their parents—that if a child wants something, the parent is going to oppose it. Of course, this is not true. An authoritative parent is not at odds with her child's interests; she is someone who seeks to embrace those interests whenever possible. Her agenda is not necessarily to deny children what they want, but help children bring their legitimate interests and projects to fruition in ways that are appropriate, effective, and responsible. By expressing honest appreciation for the goals and interests that parents feel that they can support, authoritative parents actively support their children's autonomy.

> "I love seeing you draw. Let's put your picture on the refrigerator."
>
> "You want a guitar for your birthday. I think that's a wonderful goal. If you are serious and willing to practice, I'm willing to buy you a guitar and do whatever I can to help you learn to play it well."

It is also important for parents to try to identify with some aspect of a child's interests, even when parents disagree with a child's broader goal or project.

> "You want to play football. I'm glad that you want to play a sport. You seem to enjoy it so much, and I enjoy watching you play. I'm worried about so many children getting concussions in football. Although I really want to do what I can to help you play sports, I won't have you doing something where you get hurt. Let's work on finding a way you be in a sport without getting hurt."

Over time, as children come to feel that parents have their genuine interests at heart, an emotional partnership can develop. At this point, the child and parent can begin to work together to actively advance the child's legitimate goals. As children come to see that working collaboratively with their parents succeeds in advancing their goals, they will be more likely to accept a parent's overtures and even seek a parent's guidance. A parent can facilitate the development of such a relationship by being explicit about expectations on how the child and parent can collaborate.

"I'm not here to stop you from doing the things you want. I'm here to help you figure out what you want and how to do it right. I know you want to go to Cathy's birthday party. I'd like to see you be able to go. But you can't call her up and invite yourself. If you want to have a chance to be invited to her party, what you will have to do is . . ."

Fostering the Development of Children's Autonomy

Being autonomous is to be able to do something one one's own. In this way, being autonomous is a kind of skill. We become autonomous in some activity when we have mastered the skills needed to complete it on our own. All skills take time and effort to develop. Teaching someone how to master a task—that is, how to perform autonomously in that task—occurs best through a process that psychologists call *scaffolding*. Scaffolding occurs when a parent or teacher guides a child through the process of performing a new task or acquiring a new skill. When scaffolding a child, a parent may do any or all of the following:

- Break down the task into smaller parts.
- Ask questions that direct the child's attention to parts of the task.
- Direct the child to perform individual parts of the task.
- Complete part of the task so that the child be successful another part of the task.
- Manage the child's frustration and emotional state.

Once the new skill is constructed, the parent removes the scaffolding and turns responsibility of the task over to the child. It is only at this point that a child is able to perform the task on his own—that is, autonomously.[1] For example, if a child is try-

---

1. In the world of construction, a scaffold is a raised platform used to support workers as they construct a building. When work on a given section of the building is complete, the scaffolding is removed and raised to a higher level so that the structure can be completed.

ing to put together a difficult puzzle, a parent might focus the child's attention on only part of the task. He might put two pieces together as a kind of demonstration. He might select a piece and ask, "Where does this one go?" The parent adjusts the level of support that he provides to the child's developing skill. At any point in the process, the parent supports the child's autonomy by helping the child be successful in performing that part of the task within the child's grasp. Little by little, as the child gains skill in any one part of the task, the parent relaxes the scaffolding and increasingly turns the task over to the child. At this point, the parent might up the ante and assist the child in building more complex skills.

Teaching Children to Cultivate a Sense of Self-Worth

When we think of a child's sense of self, we usually think of self-esteem. *Self-esteem* refers to a person's overall evaluation of self. It consists of one's general sense of worth and is usually expressed as an answer to the question: "How good do you feel about yourself?" Over the past 50 years or more, parents and educators have been led to believe that self-esteem is an important precondition for learning and development. As a result, parents and educators have been encouraged to praise their children's successes and protect their children from negative emotions and critical feedback, which are seen as damaging to a child's sense of self. These views are beginning to be challenged as we learn more about the dangers of overpraising children and the importance of teaching them to persevere through difficult emotion en route to success. Self-esteem isn't so much a precondition for success as it is the result of it.

Like all people, children need to develop a sense of self-

Scaffolding thus supports the work involved in constructing a building; once completed, the scaffolding is removed. Scaffolding a child's learning is a similar process.

worth. There are many was to cultivate a sense of self-worth. Ultimately, our sense of self-worth depends on our theory of who we are and who we want to be. As Carol Dweck has shown,[2] we can think of ourselves as a kind fixed thing (the fixed mindset), or we can think of ourselves as a work in progress (the growth mindset). If we are fixed things, then we are good, bad, or something in between and cannot be otherwise. However, if we are works in progress, then we are who we are becoming. If we do not like how we are right now, we are not helpless; we can do something about it. If we are works in progress, then we do not need to be threatened by our flaws and failures of the moment. Instead, we can learn to accept them as indicators that we have not yet done what we must to move closer to the person we wish to be.

Tending to Children's Need for a Worthy Sense of Self

Children need to feel loved and appreciated. The love that parents bestow on their children is foundational to a child's sense of feeling appreciated. Parents appropriately believe that it is important for them to communicate love unconditionally: "You are my child. I love you no matter what. That will never change." Such love simply cannot be communicated too often.

Loving a child unconditionally does not mean that we always love a child's behavior. While children need to feel loved and appreciated by their parents, they are nonetheless resilient beings. Parents should not feel that they cannot express disapproval for children's behavior out of a fear that children will feel unloved. Disapproval is inevitable in life and is something that children must learn to tolerate. Nonetheless, even when expressing disapproval, it is still possible to lead with appreciation: always attempt to find something that you can

---

2. Dweck, C. (2006). *Mindset: The new psychology of success.* New York: Random House.

genuinely appreciate in your child. To do so, it is necessary to separate the child from the child's action and express genuine appreciation for the child even while disapproving of the child's behavior. This can take many forms:

> "It's terrific that you've been able to wait so long for your lollipop! But you still have to wait until we get home to have it . . ."
>
> "I love the way you are able to be a good friend. When you let Ronnie play with your truck, you were being such a good friend. But it's still Ronnie's choice if he wants to keep playing with it. You can't just take it back, but you can . . ."
>
> "What I've always admired about you is your ability to give people space when they need it. But right now, you are being overwhelming to your sister!"

Fostering Self-Worth through Self-Cultivation and Self-Appreciation

All people need to feel that they have worth—that they matter. When parents lead with care and appreciation, they help provide the emotional foundation for their children's sense of self-worth. At the same time, we all have flaws; we are imperfect beings. In our life's projects, we will succeed and we will fail. In fact, it is almost inevitable that we will encounter some form of failure before we succeed. We will confront hardship, self-doubt, and difficult emotion. In fact, the capacity to persevere through failure is what allows us to overcome hardship en route to success in our life projects.

It is not possible to promote a sense of self-worth in children simply by telling them they are wonderful. Such practices bring about the very conditions that lead children to adopt a fixed mindset about their worth. The key to promoting a sense of self-worth is not bestowing esteem on children, but teaching them how to approach the task of evaluating themselves when good and bad things happen to them. This involves teaching children the skill of self-appreciation. Self-appreciation is not something that people have; it is something that people do. It is the active process of appreciating what is good about who we are in the present while simultaneously seeking to improve ourselves in the future.

Self-appreciation is an integral part of the larger process of self-cultivation (see Key 2). Recall that *self-cultivation* refers to the long, slow process of actively attempting to become the person we want to be. Fostering self-cultivation involves (1) teaching children how to adopt a growth mindset toward their skills and abilities, (2) helping children identify themselves with a system of values that defines what it means to be a good person (or to do something well), and (3) supporting children's efforts to make incremental progress toward the goal of becoming such a person. It is important to note that fostering self-cultivation is not the same as praising effort over achievement. On the contrary, fostering self-cultivation means supporting children's effort en route to achievement. Effort without achievement is a form of failure; achievement without effort typically falls far below what a child can attain with effort. With sustained effort and perseverance, children virtually always make incremental progress in their learning.

Failure is an inevitable part of learning and self-cultivation. If a child believes she has fixed abilities and qualities, then failure will necessarily result in a decline in her sense of self-worth. If my abilities are fixed, failure shows that I lack ability; as a result, my sense of self-worth declines. However, if a child defines her qualities, abilities, and skills change over time with effort and perseverance, failure is not a necessary threat to self-worth. Instead, failure simply signals that the child has not yet cultivated the desired ability, quality, or skill in question and that more perseverance, effort, and hard work are needed to do so. From this point of view, a person is a work in progress—not a series of fixed qualities.

The key to cultivating self-worth is to teach children to

actively appreciate what is good about themselves in the present (including how far they have come over time) while simultaneously looking forward to the opportunity to improve themselves. It means identifying self-worth with what is of value in who we are now and who we are becoming over time. It is the active process of identifying ours worth in terms the value in our present selves even though we know there will always be room for improvement. It does not mean ignoring or explaining away failure, difficulty, or hardship but viewing them as indicators that further effort and perseverance are necessary. This process is shown in Figure 5.2.

Because there is always room for improvement, self-appreciation also involves the knowledge that we can never fully become the persons we want to be; we can only move in the direction of our ideals. This is why identifying self-worth with who we are becoming in the present is so important. This is also why we should see humility as a part of the process of self-appreciation. If there is always room for improvement, then perfection is not possible. The awareness that we can never be perfect is an occasion for humility—the belief that there will always be something or someone who is superior to us in some way. Although humility is often seen as a sign of weakness, it is not. Humility gives us the freedom to appreciate what is good about ourselves even as we acknowledge (and

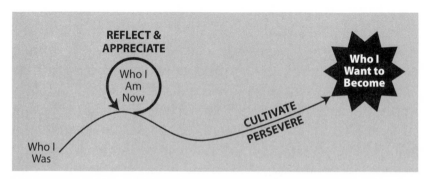

Figure 5.2. Self-Appreciation as a Part of Self-Cultivation

even celebrate) those who may be more accomplished than we are in some area of life.

To illustrate how parents can teach children how to cultivate a sense of self-worth, consider a real-life example involving a father teaching his six-year-old daughter how to snowboard.[3] Over the course of several hours, with an astonishing level of patience and skill, Annie's father taught her how to snowboard down a hill and stop effectively. He scaffolded the skills as she gradually acquired the ability to stop herself while snowboarding (self-cultivation), while also providing appreciative feedback (fostering self-appreciation) of concrete incremental changes in her skill throughout the process.

Fostering identification with a valued goal. When the day began, he announced their shared project and explicitly invited Annie to identify with it: "Annie, are you gonna learn to snowboard today?" When instructing Annie, he was careful to identify in concrete terms how to perform each action and why they were important. Explaining why stopping was important helped Annie understand why stopping was good for her. This helps her identify herself with the project of developing her skill and gives her a series of concrete image of worth to strive for.

Promoting the growth mindset. Although Annie's father does not explicitly speak of the growth mindset or the need for effort or perseverance, he does not allow his daughter to remain in a fixed mindset. Consider the following exchange (which includes Annie's mother):

MOTHER: Let's do it one more time. I want to make sure you know how to stop.

CHILD: I did stop.

FATHER: No, I stopped you on the last one.

---

3. The following examples are taken from a video of *The Kellogg Show*, www.youtube.com/watch?v=0Uc55JX32tg.

MOTHER: Stopping is really important.
FATHER: Okay?

Annie appeared to interpret her mother's suggestion that she did not yet know how to stop as a threat to her sense of worth. As a result, she defended herself by suggesting she already had the ability ("I did stop"). Her father's statement, "No, I stopped you before" communicated to Annie that she did not yet have the ability. Her mother encouraged continued practice by saying, "Stopping is really important." In situations like this, it might be even more helpful for the parent to explain the importance of effort, perseverance, and hard work in making progress.

> *"It's not big deal if you haven't learned to stop yet. It takes time to learn how to do it. But if you put the effort in, and keep at it, you'll see that you will improve. You'll be stopping on your snowboard before the day is over!"*

Teaching how to view failure as an opportunity for self-cultivation. Annie's father guided her through the process of learning to stop her snowboard. She failed many times en route to becoming proficient. Although Annie's father never criticized her ability, called her names, or characterized her in any negative way, he did not refrain from providing sensitive, clear, and honest feedback. With each failure, Annie's father patiently explained what she was doing wrong and provided instructions and guidance for how to improve:

> *[As Annie slides down hill] "Stand up! Hands all the way up! Heels, heels, heels!" [Child falls] "See what I mean, you have to really push hard on your heels."*

Some parents have been led to believe that providing children with corrective feedback is damaging to a child's self-esteem. Criticizing a child's ability (i.e., "you're no good at snowboarding," "you don't have the aptitude for this") is damaging to a child's sense of self. It actually teaches a child to adopt a fixed mindset. It leads the child to believe that his success or failure in any task is a function of some sort of fixed inner ability and communicates to a child that he does not have the ability in question. There is a great difference, however, between criticizing a child's abilities and providing corrective feedback to support continued improvement. The former teaches a child that he has fixed worth; the latter teaches the child how to cultivate new skills over time.

Acknowledging incremental progress. At one point, in teaching Annie how to stop herself, holding her hands to steady her, Annie's father guided her down the hill as he coached her on how to dig in her heels to stop the snowboard. As Annie made small improvements, her father calmly praised each new step, "That's the way, that's the way." This helps the child gain immediate feedback about the fate of her efforts. She is able to see that she is able to make immediate (if gradual) progress when she puts forth effort and follows her father's guidance.

Learning to identify value in oneself in the present. Annie's parents encouraged her to appreciate her present worth in many ways. After the day was over, Annie's father expressed his appreciation for his daughter's progress by saying, "You are going so much faster now!" This encourages Annie to compare herself to her previous performance and reflect on how far she has come.

Self-appreciation is an important step in the process of learning how to cultivate a worthy sense of self. However, this step is not something that can be performed in isolation; it is part of the larger process of self-cultivation. Cultivating self-worth is not a simple product of looking at one's self and finding that one is good or bad. Instead, cultivating a sense of self-worth is a skill that develops over timeand is thus something we can teach our children to do. To foster the skill of self-appreciation, when issues related to self-worth arise, teach children to stop, reflect, and find the value in who they are or what they have done in

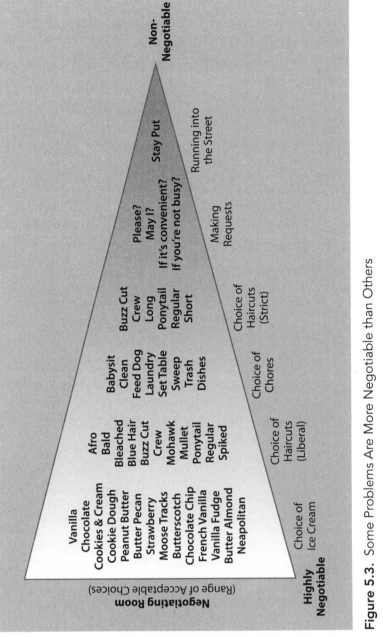

Figure 5.3. Some Problems Are More Negotiable than Others

the present. Quite often children will judge themselves by making comparisons to other children, noting their success or failure in school or in some task, or reacting to someone's opinion. At this point, it is important to remind children that their worth is to found in the incremental progress they make in working effortfully toward their goals. Our task to define ourselves in terms of the value we find in who we are now, in how far we have come over time, and in our continued willingness to improve ourselves in the future.

Task 5.1. Fostering Self-Cultivation and Self-Appreciation

Fostering autonomy, self-appreciation, and growth through perseverance are all parts of the process of self-cultivation. The important word here is *process*. Our skills, abilities, and sense of self-worth are not fixed things but are processes that are developing over time. The moment we begin to think of ourselves as processes and not things, everything changes, for we realize that we must work at becoming who we want to become. If this is true, then developing a sense of self-worth is something that is always in process—it is something we *do*—even something we can choose; it is not something that we simply have.

To learn to cultivate appreciation for our selves, we need to reflect on how far we have come since yesterday even as we plan to improve ourselves tomorrow. When we do this, we realize that we will almost inevitably have made some progress—however small—in who we are trying to become. At that point, we can stop and actively appreciate—deliberately seek value—in what is valuable about ourselves today and in the present moment. The process looks like the following.

When we encourage our children to think in this way, we help them identify valued goals in life (e.g., My Big Goal). Of course, even as we strive to move toward our goals, perfection is always (necessarily) beyond our reach. We come to terms with this when we are able to accept our imperfections, appreciate who we are now, and still strive to become better. You can use the chart below to reflect on and appreciate your efforts at self-cultivation, as well as to think about how to guide your child in doing so.

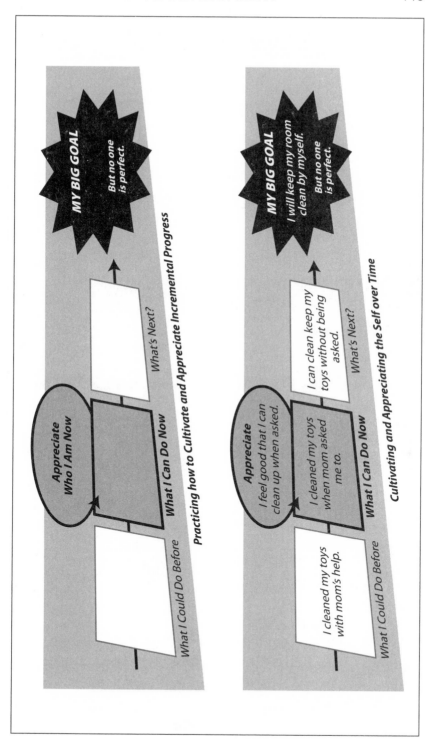

Practicing how to Cultivate and Appreciate Incremental Progress

MY BIG GOAL — But no one is perfect.

Appreciate Who I Am Now

What I Can Do Now

What's Next?

What I Could Do Before

Cultivating and Appreciating the Self over Time

MY BIG GOAL — I will keep my room clean by myself. But no one is perfect.

Appreciate — I feel good that I can clean up when asked.

What I Can Do Now — I cleaned my toys when mom asked me to.

What's Next? — I can clean keep my toys without being asked.

What I Could Do Before — I cleaned my toys with mom's help.

SOLVE PROBLEMS

Good things happen when we think of conflict as an opportunity for problem solving.

As children develop, the first step to authoritative parenting is to establish a responsive yet directive relationship between parents and children. This requires acknowledging and tending to children's emotional needs while simultaneously setting high expectations and clear limits. The preceding chapters describe a variety of ways parents can be loving and emotionally supportive while teaching children to respect rules and parental interests. As children grow older, they become able participate in increasingly sophisticated interactions with their parents and peers. They begin to seek increasing levels of autonomy and can shoulder increasing levels of responsibility.

As this happens, the next step of authoritative parenting can begin. Over time, it becomes possible to engage children in increasingly collaborative interactions, even around issues related to discipline. While being mindful of their responsibility to guide and direct their children's development, parents can begin to invite children to play increasingly active roles in decisions that involve them. One particularly effective way to support the development of children's autonomy while simultaneously providing sensitive guidance is to involve children in the process of guided collaboration and problem solving. Guided collaboration occurs when parents and children work together to solve problems and resolve conflicts for the mutual gain of children and parents. Guided collaboration is a form of conflict management that can be used between parents and children. When practicing guided collaboration, parents use actual everyday conflict (between parents and children, among children) as teaching moments. Using the conflict management steps described next, the parent guides the child through a problem-solving process—namely, the process of finding ways to resolve the interpersonal conflict that advance the interests of both parents and children. Using guided problem solving, parents work with children to help them advance their legitimate interests while simultaneously advancing the parent's standards, principles, and rules.

What Is Conflict?

Conflict refers to any kind of opposition that exists between two things. Conflict can arise between parents and children or between children. By definition, a child's misbehavior is a kind of conflict—the child's behavior conflicts with an adult's standards, desires, or rules. Toni's failure to say "please" conflicts with her grandmother's standards for polite behavior. Sam's messy room violates his mother's desire for tidiness. Edwin's delaying tactics conflict with his parent's rule that he honor his bedtime (see Table 6.1).

However, not all conflicts between parents and children are related to rules. We sometimes forget, for example, that parents have interests and needs too. Quite often, children's needs and desires come into conflict with those of their parents (see Table 6.2). A child may want to be taken to a friend's house to play,

Table 6.1. Child's Behavior Conflicts with Parent's Rule

Child's Behavior	Conflicts With	Parent's Rule
Not saying "please"		"Use your manners."
Having toys on the floor		"Keep your room clean."
Trying to stay up later		"Bedtime!"

Table 6.2. Child's Desires Conflict with Parent's Interests

Child's Desires	Conflicts With	Parent's Interests
Can you take me to a friend's?		I'm enjoying my bath
Read the book again!		I'm tired!
Can I use the computer?		I'm checking my email.

but Mom wants to take a bath. A child might want her mother to read her a book for the fifth consecutive time, but Dad is exhausted. Ruth may want to play on the computer, but her mother is checking her email.

Among children, conflicts happen all the time. Conflicts between children sometimes involve violations of parental rules and standards (e.g., aggressive behavior, taking property, being disrespectful) (see Table 6.3).

However, not all conflicts between children involve rule violations. Many conflicts between children have to do with competing desires and interests, such as conflicts about how to spend playtime, how to play a game, and who should go first in line (see Table 6.4).

Some conflicts lend themselves to guided collaboration and problem solving better than others. The process is effective for most types of conflicts that occur between and among parents and children. As active participants in the process of guided problem solving, children learn how to express their own interests while simultaneously taking into consideration the needs and interests of others.

As already discussed, a conflict is any type of opposition that

Table 6.3. Child's Behavior Conflicts with Parent's Rule Regarding Others

Child's Behavior	Conflicts With	Parent's Rule
Nora hits Tim		"No hitting."
Tim takes Nora's toys		"Ask permission first"
Calling each other names		"Be respectful."

Table 6.4. Children's Competing Desires

Nora's Desire	Conflicts With	Tim's Desire
Let's play "hospital."		Let's make a video!
I want to be the doctor!		You be the patient!
I want to be first in line!		I want to be first in line!

can occur between two people. As discussed throughout this book, children and adults are not equals. Not all conflicts between parents and children are occasions for negotiation. Some parental rules are not negotiable: there can be no negotiation with a preschooler about wandering near traffic, swimming in deep water, or playing with fire. As shown in Figure 5.3, conflict between parents and children can range from the highly negotiable (e.g., differences in opinion about what flavor of ice cream to serve at a party) to the nonnegotiable (e.g., conflicts that relate to a child's safety and well-being). More highly negotiable issues have greater range of possible outcomes (negotiating room) than do less negotiable issues. It is the responsibility of the parent, of course, to determine the types of conflicts that are open for negotiation. Negotiable problems lend themselves to guided problem solving; less negotiable ones must be managed using other disciplinary strategies (see Keys 1 and 4). Of course, parents differ in what they regard as acceptable topics and areas for guided problem solving. For example, as was shown back in Figure 5.3, some parents may endorse a broader range of possible haircuts (more liberal) for their children than others (more strict).

Four Ways of Resolving Conflict

A conflict is a type of problem. Where conflict arises between people, the problem becomes one of how to manage or resolve it. If Nora wants to play "hospital" and Tim wants to make a video, they have a problem. How can they manage or eliminate the conflict between their positions? It Nora and Tim have opposing positions, how can that opposition be transformed or otherwise eliminated? If there is distance between Nora and Tim, how can they reduce that distance? This is what it means to say that a conflict is a type of problem. The trick is to view conflict as a kind of problem to be solved rather than as an insurmountable obstacle. The problem then becomes one of reducing the distance between opposing positions.

Conflicts between people can be resolved in three basic ways. These include win-lose, compromise, and mutual gain (win-win solutions). The win-lose solution is based on the idea that negotiating conflict is a zero-sum game, in which only one person can win, and his wins are equal to the other person's losses. From this view, conflict is understood as a kind of competition in which only one person can win. When this occurs, the process of managing conflict becomes a kind of power struggle. The person with the most power wins—whether that power takes the form of authority, persuasive force, physical force, or some other resource.

Between parents and children, the win-lose solutions can take two basic forms. In the first, the parent wins and the child loses. Here is an example.

MOM: It's raining out—be sure to wear your raincoat!

JESSE: I hate that raincoat. I'm not wearing it.

MOM: What do you mean you hate that raincoat? It keeps you dry! That's what a raincoat is for!

JESSE: It's ugly and I don't want to wear it.

MOM: That's too bad. Put your raincoat on or you're not going to the party tonight.

JESSE: You're mean!

In this situation, the mother wins and Jesse loses. The mother uses the power of her authority and her capacity to punish Jesse to force her to put on the raincoat. The mother's concern, of course, is valid. She wants Jesse to be warm and dry. Wearing a raincoat is a good solution to this problem. The question of what young children should and should not wear on cold days is certainly within the sphere of a parent's legitimate authority. Nonetheless, there may be other ways besides blind power assertion to enforce the parent's rule and solve the problem of keeping Jesse warm.

In the second form of the win-lose solution, the child wins and the parent loses. Here is an example of how that can happen.

Mom: It's raining out—be sure to wear your raincoat!

Jesse: I hate that raincoat. I'm not wearing it.

Mom: What do you mean you hate that raincoat? It's a beautiful raincoat! You loved that raincoat!

Jesse: It's ugly and I don't want to wear it.

Mom: Oh, come on. It's not such a bad raincoat. If you don't wear it, you're going to get your new blouse all wet. I think you should wear it.

Jesse: Well, I'm not wearing it.

Mom: Oh come on, wear it. Please?

Jesse: I'm not wearing it!

Mom: Fine. Suit yourself.

In this situation, Jesse's mother essentially relinquishes her parental authority. The situation unfolds as a power struggle, except the child has all of the power. As a result, Jesse's mother adopts the stance of trying to convince Jesse to wear the raincoat. When that fails, she resorts to pleading. This is a common type of interaction that occurs often between permissive parents and their children. In situations like this, permissive parents often become frustrated and begin to move back and forth between demanding and pleading.

The third way to resolve conflict is compromise. Compromise is also based on the idea that managing conflict is a zero-sum game. However, instead of resulting in a situation in which one person wins and one person loses, both partners get part of what was wanted, and both concede something that is not wanted. Here is an example of a compromise between Jesse and her mother.

Mom: It's raining out—be sure to wear your raincoat!

Jesse: I hate that raincoat. I'm not wearing it.

Mom: I didn't know that you hated that coat. Still, I want you to wear it. It keeps you warm and dry.

Jesse: But all the kids are gonna laugh at me if they see me wearing it. Please don't make me wear it.

Mom: Wear the raincoat to school, and then take it off when you get into the building.

Jesse: But the kids will see me on the bus. I'll take it off when I get on the bus.

Mom: Okay, but only if you put it on again before you get off the bus.

Jesse: Argh. Okay, but they're gonna see my stupid coat when I put it back on.

Mom: Well, I would still prefer that you wore it until you get to school.

Jesse: Okay, I'll put it back on when I get off the bus.

Mom: Promise?

Jesse: Yes.

In this situation, both Jesse and her mother get a portion of what each wanted, but also give up something. As a result, neither is particularly happy with the outcome. Neither Jesse's nor her mother's interests have been fully addressed. Jesse's mother knows this; that is why she is not confident that Jesse will fulfill her end of the bargain. Once Jesse is outside of her mother's sight, she will have the choice of whether to wear her coat.

Because Jesse's interests have not been fully acknowledged and addressed, she is not fully invested in the agreement that she made with her mother. They remain at odds.

The fourth way to manage or resolve interpersonal conflict is to seek solutions for mutual gain, sometimes called win-win solutions. Creating win-win solutions becomes possible when people begin to realize that conflict need not be a zero-sum game. There is no reason to think of interpersonal conflict as competition in which only one person can win. For most problems that occur between people, there are solutions that can allow both partners to advance their interests and get what they want. The gains of one partner do not have come at the expense of the other. Both partners can gain simultaneously. Here is an example of a win-win solution between Jesse and her mother.

MOM: Jesse, it's raining out. Don't forget to wear your raincoat!

JESSE: I don't want to wear a raincoat!

MOM: You don't want your raincoat? Why not?

JESSE: I don't need one!

MOM: You don't need one? But it's pouring out! There must be some other reason you don't want to wear your raincoat!

JESSE: I hate that raincoat. The last time I wore that raincoat, everyone called me names!

MOM: Goodness! That must have been embarrassing. But we've got a problem here. I don't want you to get wet, and you don't want the kids to make fun of you. Is there some way that we can prevent you from getting wet and not have the kids make fun of you?

JESSE: Well, you know, I kinda like your blue jacket.

MOM: You mean my old blue jacket with the rip in the sleeve? I didn't know you liked that old thing. I think it looks awful! But if you like it, you can have it!

JESSE: Gee, thanks Mom!

In this win-win solution to the raincoat dilemma, both Jesse and her mother are able to advance their interests. Jesse's mother is able to advance her interest of keeping her daughter warm and dry; Jesse is able to advance her interest of not looking stupid (and even, perhaps, looking rather cool in her mother's retro slicker). The solution removes the conflict between Jesse and her mother and allows each to advance her interests.

The Key to Win-Win Solutions: Separate Interests from Positions

The most important aspect of managing conflict through the process of guided problem solving involves separating *interests* from *positions*. Let's return to Jesse and her raincoat. Jesse's mother wanted her to wear her raincoat, but Jesse didn't want to it because she feared she might look silly in front of her friends. In the win-lose versions of this conflict, Jesse and her mother staked out two separate and opposing *positions*.

MOM: "Wear your raincoat."

JESSE: "I won't wear my raincoat."

A position is a kind of stance that a person takes on an issue. When we take a position on an issue, we are saying, "This is what I believe," "This is what should be," or "This is what I'm going to do." There is no room for debate. When people hold two opposing positions on an issue, the options for resolving the conflict are limited. Either one person wins and the other loses, or both compromise and neither gets all of what was wanted. To stake out a position is to commit oneself to a particular belief or course of action; the person becomes emotionally invested in his position: "This is *my* position." As a result, in a fight over positions, a person's sense of self is at stake. To give in is a sign of weakness; to be compelled to give up one's position is a source of shame, humiliation, and resentment.

Figure 6.1. Conflicting Positions

When Jesse and her mother stake out inflexible positions, they immediately become locked in a power struggle—a zero-sum game in which Jesse can only gain ground if her mother loses ground and vice versa. Most conflicts are fights over positions. However, what happened in the win-win version of the conflict between Jesse and her mother? How were they able to resolve their dispute? How did the win-win scenario differ from the win-lose and compromise solutions?

What is the nature of the *conflict* that occurs between Jesse and her mother? Where do they disagree? In the win-lose and compromise versions of the conflict, they disagree over whether Jesse should wear her raincoat. They have adopted conflicting positions (see Figure 6.1).

Why do Jesse and her mother adopt the positions that they do? What are the interests that motivate them? What problems are each trying to solve? If we look beneath the positions that Jesse and her mother take, can we tell what each person really wants in this situation? What is each trying to achieve? Asking these questions will allow Jesse and her mother to separate their interests from their positions. This is an essential step in the process of managing and resolving conflict between individuals.

In the win-win version of the conflict, we find that Jesse's interest is to avoid looking foolish in front of her friends. Her mother's interest is to ensure that Jesse stays warm and dry (see Figure 6.2).

With respect to the question of whether she should wear a raincoat, Jesse's position is in conflict with her mother's position. However, there is not necessarily a conflict between what Jesse and her mother really want in this situation—their inter-

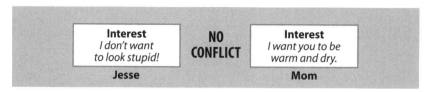

Figure 6.2. Nonconflicting Interests

ests. Jesse's mother's interest is for Jesse to be warm and dry; Jesse's interest is to avoid looking foolish by wearing the raincoat.

We can now begin to understand the nature of the conflict. Jesse adopts her position ("I don't want to wear the raincoat") on the basis of her interest ("I don't want to look foolish; that raincoat will make me look foolish"). Jesse's mother adopts her position ("I want you to wear your raincoat") on the basis of her interest (she wants Jesse to be warm and dry). Here we see that although their positions on the issue of wearing a raincoat conflict, the interests that motivate those conflicting positions are not necessarily in conflict (Figure 6.3)

Once Jesse and her mother identify their genuine interests, they can begin the process of finding solutions that will advance their interests at the same time.

Work from Interests, Not Positions

Once they separate their positions from their interests, Jesse's mother can now guide Jesse—often without Jesse even knowing—through the process of collaborative problem solving.

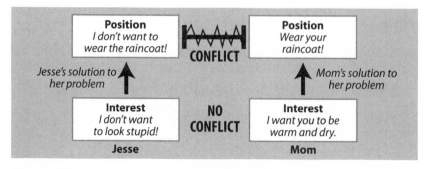

Figure 6.3. Focus on Interests to Find Solutions

The key at this point is to focus on interests—not positions. After all, our interests are what really matter; our positions are merely way stations en route to getting our interests met. If Jesse and her mother have successfully identified their genuine interests, they will feel less defensive as they work together to consider alternative ways of meeting those interests. Thus, in any situation, once parents and children have identified their genuine interests, they can move on to the problem of how to manage or resolve the conflict between those interests. The basic question becomes: how can we invent a solution to this problem that advances both of our interests?

Because Jesse's genuine interests were not in conflict with her mother's genuine interests, they were able to resolve their conflict by inventing a win-win solution that advanced both of their interests simultaneously. Jesse was able to look fashionable while her mother was assured that her daughter would be warm and dry. Although they worked together to resolve the conflict, Jesse's mother was able to address Jesse's interests without giving in on her own interests. Although Jesse's mother was open to alternative ways of advancing her interests, her primary interest—that Jesse be warm and dry—was nonnegotiable. If Jesse and her mother focused only on their positions—their initial solutions to the problems that they were trying to solve— they would have failed to reach a win-win solution. When they were able to focus on their genuine interests, they were able to see multiple ways to reach their goals. By working to find solutions that advanced both of their interests simultaneously, the pair was able to invent a win-win solution.

Steps in Guided Problem Solving Between Parents and Children

You can guide your child through the process of collaborative problem solving by following the following steps. However, remember that real life is messy. Despite our best intentions, real life problem solving rarely follows a fixed sequence. More often than not, you'll find yourself jumping back and forth between the various steps. In any case, it's never a good idea to follow a rigid script. Don't be afraid to innovate and follow your instincts!

Step 1: Calm Down

The first step to guided problem solving is sometimes the hardest: calmness. When was the last time that you had a successful collaboration when one or both partners were angry or upset in some way? If you are like most of us, the answer is most likely "never."

It is virtually impossible to engage in successful collaborative problem solving if anyone involved in the collaboration is overly upset. When a child misbehaves, or when there is some sort of conflict, anger and frustration are natural reactions. This is true of both parents and children.

When someone is angry at you, he has made the judgment that you have done something wrong. As result, the angry person will attempt to move against the alleged wrongdoer in an attempt to change that person's behavior. If I am angry at you, I am likely to blame you for what you did. When I blame you, you are likely to become defensive and blame me back. The cycle escalates. There prevents effective problem solving.

The same is true if people are afraid. When a parent gets angry, a child is likely to experience some degree of fear. When a child is afraid, she is most likely to try to avoid further contact with the parent. She will do anything to get away from the angry person. Have you ever tried to engage in problem solving with someone when you felt afraid of them? The result is that you tend to tell the angry person what they want to hear rather than what you really think. That is not a formula for success.

The first steps are to calm everyone down. How can this be done?

- **Identify the situation as a teaching and learning moment.** Rather than thinking of a child as doing something wrong, the parent thinks of the situation as one in which a child needs to learn new skills. Quite often, simply reframing misbehavior as a teaching opportunity is enough to bring a parent from upset to in control.

- **Wait until you are calm.** Try to calm yourself down. If you are too angry or upset to engage your children, make sure the situation is under control and defer problem solving until later.
- **Calm your children down.** If your children are upset, wait until they are calm before you engage in guided collaboration. Sometimes this is as simple as asking them to calm down. Engage the emotional modulation principles and strategies discussed elsewhere in this book.
- **"Nothing happens until you are calm."** Sometimes, children can be demanding when there is a mishap or misbehavior: "Jonah hit me!" "He started it!" "That's not fair!" This is not the time for problem solving. An effective strategy for calming children in these situations is simply to say, "Nothing happens until you are calm." Then mean it: simply stop all action and do nothing until everyone is calm. You'll be surprised at how quickly children can calm themselves when they know that getting what they want is at stake.
- **Have everyone take a break or a time out until everyone is calm.** Today, a time out is often used as a punishment: "If you don't stop that, you'll get a time out!" That's *not* a time out. A time out is simply a break from the situation to allow everyone to calm down and reflect on the situation. Once everyone is calm, collaborative problem solving can begin.

Step 2: Identify Everyone's Genuine Interests

After everyone is calm, it is time to identify the interests of each person involved in the conflict. This is a crucial step. The most important part of this step is to separate interests from positions.

Separating interests from positions is not something that comes naturally. It is up to the parent to help a child express his real goals and wants. In so doing, it is often helpful to think of your task as trying to figure out the problem your child is trying to solve. Children will not always be able to tell you what their real interests and goals are, at least not right away. One way to help them articulate their interests is to assure them that you are genuinely concerned about their interests—that, if at all possible, you want to find a way to actually help them meet their interests. Of course, you have to really mean it; children will know immediately when a parent is feigning interest to manipulate a child into something. You can say something like, "If at all possible, I really want to help you get what you want. But I can't do that unless you tell me what it is."

Paradoxically, one way to help children articulate their interests is to back off a bit. When there is a conflict between a child and a parent, the natural inclination is to oppose the child's position. Try to avoid this. Children will be more likely to open up if they feel that their feelings and perspectives will be heard and understood (even if a parent may not agree with what a child might say). Children—like adults—are less likely to express themselves if they feel judged or otherwise anticipate that a parent will disapprove of how they feel. One way to communicate acceptance and encourage children to speak is simply to acknowledge what a child says in a supportive or nonjudgmental way. For example, after Jesse refused to wear her raincoat, her mother acknowledged her sentiment by saying, "You don't want to wear your raincoat." Quite often, simply reflecting back what a child has said is enough to prompt him or her to begin to talk. Alternatively, a parent can ask open-ended questions about the problem. Jesse's mother did so while communicating genuine concern about Jesse's interests, "Why don't you want to wear your raincoat?" and "There must be some other reason you don't want to wear your raincoat!"

Task 6.1. Identifying Interests

Identifying interests is the first step to resolving conflicts. It is important to identify not only the interests (goals, motives, desires, and wants) that motivate your child's misbehavior but also necessary your own. When a child misbehaves, although we may be aware that we don't approve of something that the child has done, we are often not immediately aware of exactly why we disapprove. For example, you notice that your child's room is a mess and want him to clean it up. Your immediate position is that your child should clean his room. Why? Is it because you are embarrassed that your child's room is a mess? Because you want your child to learn to be responsible for cleaning? Because a messy room bothers you in some other way? Whatever the case, you can't work toward a win-win solution with your child unless you know what your genuine interests are and why you have them.

The same is true for your child. When we focus only on a child's behavior (i.e., your child runs away and hides to avoid cleaning him room) without considering the interests and concerns that motivate the child's misbehavior, the usual course of action is to use our power to force our children to do what we want. Power assertion by itself does not lead to long-lasting behavioral change. Why isn't my child cleaning his room? Is it because he is overwhelmed with the task? Does he just want to play and doesn't care about cleaning? Is he afraid that he will do it wrong and you will yell at him? Your response to a child's behavior will vary depending on your understanding of the interests that motivate it. More important, the only way to create win-win solutions to interpersonal conflict is to understand your child's interests.

Understanding a child's interests does not come easily. Use the right panel of the diagram to reflect on the interests that motivate you and your child in typical conflicts that occur in your home. The more you practice—before and during a conflict situation—the better you will get.

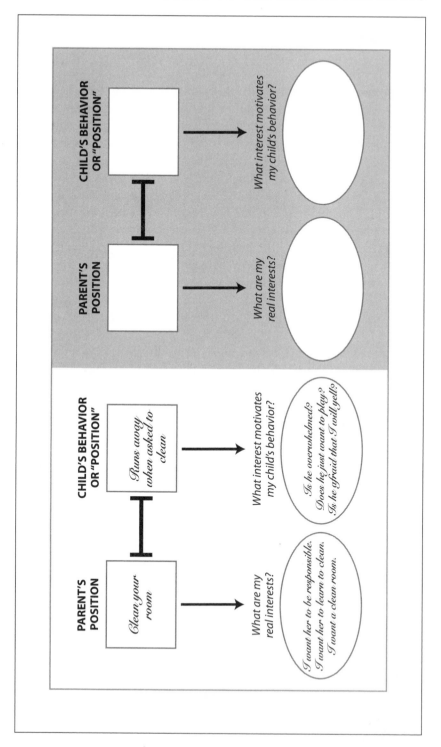

Step 3: Brainstorm Solutions for Mutual Gain: Good Ones, Bad Ones, and Ugly Ones

Once you have identified the interests (problems and goals) of each person in the conflict (and have separated them from each person's positions), it is time to brainstorm. Each person involved in the conflict can work to generate as many possible solutions to the conflict as possible. Your goal is to generate win-win solutions—solutions that advance the interest of each person in the conflict, without giving in on the parent's core interests.

As you generate solutions, it is important to solicit and entertain all types of solutions—good solutions, bad solutions, and even ugly solutions. This is a very important point. We are most interested in inventing "good" (win-win) solutions. However, bad solutions and even ugly solutions are important as well. They are important for many reasons,

Sometimes bad solutions are really good solutions. Sometimes people don't suggest solutions because they think the ideas are stupid or will make them look stupid. Accepting (or even inviting!) bad solutions solves this problem. For example, Jesse might suggest that she can be warm and dry without wearing her raincoat if she could wear her old brown coat—the one that Mom knows is too small for her. This sounds like a bad idea, as her mother has already banished the brown coat. However, because it *would* keep her warm and dry—and this is Jesse's mother's primary interest in the context, this suggestion might be workable—at least temporarily. Her mother might reject Jesse's solution; but she might not.

Sometimes bad solutions lead to good solutions. Imagine that Jesse's mother rejected the old brown coat solution. Suggesting the old coat could have the effect of getting the pair to think about what other types of clothes Jesse can wear instead of the old coat (like her mother's retro jacket). If this were to happen, a bad solution could lead to a good solution.

Ugly ideas help clarify what is really not acceptable and

why. Imagine that Jesse suggested that she might be able to keep dry if, instead of having to wait for the bus, her mother drove her to school. Now, this is a rather ugly idea because it would require her mother to go out of her way to take Jesse to school when this is not necessary. It would also not solve the problem of how Jesse is going to keep dry on the way home. This solution is not very considerate of Jesse's mother. However, evaluating the ugly idea is a teaching moment. It is clear that Jesse does not know why it is so ugly. Explaining why the idea doesn't work clarifies what is at stake in the conflict. For example, Jesse can't advance her interests at the cost of her mother's; she must solve the problem of keeping dry all day.

Task 6.2. Brainstorming Possibilities

In a situation involving conflict between you and your child, after you have identified each other's genuine interests, it's time to try to invent ways to resolve your conflict and meet each other's (legitimate) interests. Imagine that you have asked your son why he is avoiding cleaning his room. After saying, "I don't know" and then making up some irrelevant excuses ("I forgot"; "I don't have time"), you are able to help him get closer to the real issue. He says, "Cleaning up my room is too much work!" Assuming that you, the parent, have good reasons (your own interests) for wanting your child to clean his room, the choice of not cleaning his room will not be available to your child. The question then becomes, "How can I advance my interest to have my child clean his room while simultaneously being sensitive to his (naive) concern that cleaning is too much work?" Showing sensitivity to the child's concern, the parent can say something like, "So, you feel that cleaning the room is too much work. Are there things we can do to make cleaning your room easier?" Help your child think up both good and bad solutions to the problem. There are many ways a child can lighten the burden of cleaning his room. Asking for help, taking breaks, and running and hiding are three possible solutions. Although some solutions are better than others, at this point, it's important simply to brainstorm possible solutions — good and bad — without evaluating them (that will be the next step). This is shown in the left panel of the figure. Use the right panel to brainstorm possible ways your child can meet his interests in the conflict(s) that you considered in Task 6.1.

Keep in mind that this process does not just apply to your child — it also applies to you! Yes, your core interests are nonnegotiable. There are usually ways that you have not yet thought of that you can advance your interests, even when they are nonnegotiable. (Sometimes, parents find that their interests actually change, or aspects of those interests might be negotiable. For example, in reflection, a parent might come to see that it is important to her that her child clean his room but not make the bed or organize the contents of his dresser.) Some possible ways to advance a parent's goal of teaching her child to be responsible for a clean room are listed in the diagram. You can use the right panel to brainstorm alternative ways you can advance your interests in real-life conflicts that occur in your home.

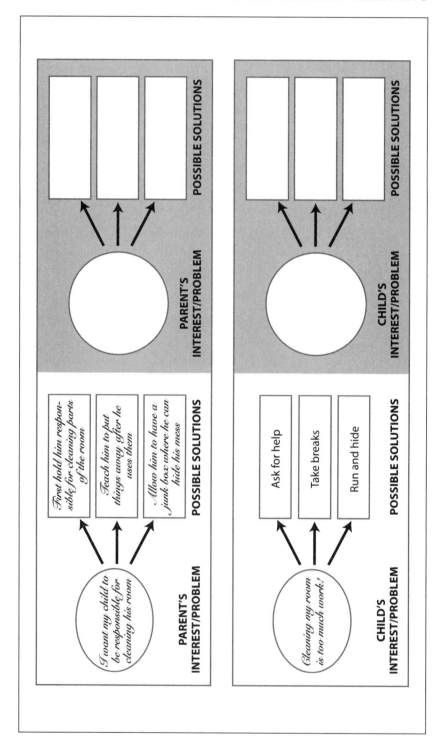

Task 6.3. What Will Work? What Won't?

In attempting to work out a win-win solution, it is sometimes helpful to guide children through the process of evaluating the pros and cons of various ways of solving a problem. For example, ask a child to imagine the consequences of the different ways she has suggested for solving a problem or advancing interests. This is shown in the left panel of the diagram. A parent might ask, "What are the positive and negative things that could happen if you ask for help? Take breaks? Run and hide?" Guiding your child through this process helps her understand the effects that her behavior has on other people. It also helps her understand that positive and negative aspects of making poor choices (e.g., running and hiding). You can use the panel on the right to explore the effects of different possible solutions to conflicts that arise in your own home.

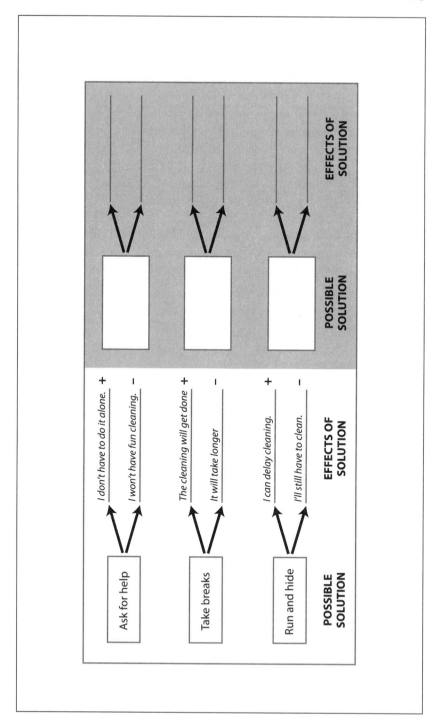

POSSIBLE
SOLUTION

EFFECTS OF
SOLUTION

Ask for help

- I don't have to do it alone. +
- I won't have fun cleaning. −

Take breaks

- The cleaning will get done +
- It will take longer −

Run and hide

- I can delay cleaning. +
- I'll still have to clean. −

POSSIBLE
SOLUTION

EFFECTS OF
SOLUTION

Step 4: Select Solutions Together
and Take Shared Responsibility

After a set of possible solutions has been proposed—hopefully by everyone involved in the conflict—then it's time to evaluate them and jointly choose a course of action. The task is to select the solution that best advances the interests of both child and parent, without the parent giving in. It is sometimes useful (particularly with older children) to list the proposed solutions and evaluate their strengths and weaknesses. To illustrate, Table 6.5 lists pros and cons of various solutions to Jesse's problem. Although it is possible to make tables and drawings to help young children evaluates pros and cons, they must be adjusted for the child's age and developmental level. (Strategies for helping young children evaluate possible solutions to shared problems are discussed in further detail in Key 7.)

This table can give a sense of the range of different solutions that might be proposed for any given problem (from the good through the bad to the ugly), as well as how each solution has

Table 6.5. Evaluating Solutions

Solution	Pro	Con
Jesse could wear no coat	• Jesse avoids looking unfashionable	• Jesse won't stay dry as her mother wants
Jesse could wear her raincoat	• Jesse stays warm and dry • Jesse learns to cope with looking unfashionable	• Jesse looks unfashionable • Jesse won't like wearing the coat
Jesse could bring an umbrella	• Jesse likes umbrellas • Jesse looks fashionable	• Jesse will be cold
Mom can drive Jesse to school	• Jesse gets to stay warm and dry in the morning	• Mom has to go out of her way • Jesse won't be warm and dry coming home from school
Jesse can wear Mom's old retro coat	• Jesse is warm and dry • Jesse will look fashionable	• Jesse doesn't learn how to cope with wearing a coat she doesn't like

both positive and negative points. Only the last solution adequately advances both Jesse's and her mother's interests. Even this solution has a downside (Jesse won't learn to tolerate wearing a raincoat). If learning to tolerate the raincoat were one of Jesse's mom's primary interests, this solution might not be feasible.

It's not over yet! This is because both Jesse and her mother must now take shared *responsibility* for the outcomes of the decision that they have made together. Since both Jesse and her mother agreed to the solution, neither Jesse nor her mother can blame the other if the solution turns out badly. Jesse cannot say, "You made me wear this coat, and everyone laughed at me!"; Jesse's mother cannot say, "You got wet anyway—I told you to wear the other coat!" This last point is more of an issue with older children, but it is also relevant for young children. Ivan wants to play both checkers and Monopoly, but his father says that he can choose only one. Given the choice between the two (and being forewarned), Ivan cannot try one and then come back and say, "Monopoly is too hard—can I have checkers instead?"

Viewing Discipline as the Resolution of Parent–Child Conflict

Situations in which children engage in misbehavior can often be treated as opportunities for resolving conflict. This is because a child's misbehavior is essentially a type of conflict between the parent and the child. The key to understanding how discipline can be a form of conflict resolution is to remember that the goal of conflict resolution is to seek win-win solutions between parents and children without parents giving in. Managing conflict between parents and children is not about saying things nicely, seeking compromise, or bargaining over positions. Conflict resolution is about advancing a parent's interests and standards firmly in ways that are also sensitive to a child's needs.

Frankly, a parent should always feel in control in her interactions with children. When parents do not feel in control, it is usually because they fear that their children will not follow their directives. This tends to happen in two situations. The first occurs when children of authoritarian parents rebel against coercive parenting strategies. The second occurs when permissive parents fail to impose limits that are fully within the parent's control. When parents fail to impose limits, they often feel as though they have to convince, cajole, or persuade their children to follow their directives. When parents get to the point that they feel the need to persuade or plead, it is usually an indication that they have failed to impose limits that are within their control—that is, that they have given in on their core interests and standards.

Many parents fear that since children can always refuse to comply with a parental directive, a parent's influence over a child is limited. In one sense, this is true—a parent never directly control his child's behavior. The only behavior that a parent can exert direct control over is his own. However, this is all a parent needs! Although parents cannot control their children's behavior, they can exert a profound influence over their children's behavior by choosing how they will respond to the choices their children make. Parents can influence their children by acting in ways that force children to adapt to the parent's behavior. A child may refuse to eat her dinner. Although the parent cannot force the child to eat, the parent still has the choice of deciding how he will respond to the child's refusal. The child's refusal, for example, does not mean that the parent needs to cook her something different. When the parent refuses to cook something different, the child is forced to adapt to the parent's choices. For example, the child can either make a bowl of cereal or go to bed hungry.

In this way, managing conflict with children doesn't put the parent in a position of weakness. Quite the opposite—the parent who refuses to give in on her interests (but is willing to negotiate positions) retains full control over how to respond to a child's choice making. A parent who learns this will rarely experience a sense of lacking control in her interactions with children.

Tables 6.6–6.9 offer some examples of conflict management

Table 6.6. Dinner Time

Conversation	Comment
Dad: "Eat your peas."	Father makes demand.
Jen: I hate peas. I don't want to eat them.	Child expresses her interest and feeling.
Dad: Peas are good for you. You have to have your vegetables.	Father begins ineffectively by trying to convince Jen that she should eat her peas. He begins to express his interest, but is not yet clear in doing so.
Jen: I hate peas. I won't eat them.	Jen states her position—she won't eat her peas.
Dad: You don't like peas. What kind of vegetable do you like?	Father does not address Jen's position, but instead focuses on his interest (to have her eat nutritious vegetables) and her interest (perhaps there are vegetables that she likes).
Jen: I like corn. And cooked carrots.	Jen offers two solutions that would advance both her own and her father's interests.
Dad: Sounds good, but I'm not going to cook you something else. You can either cook some vegetables for yourself, or eat some raw carrots.	Father identifies an additional personal interest—hat he does not want to cook something new just for Jen. He suggests another solution—eat raw carrots.
Jen: I like cooked carrots.	Jen states her position.
Dad: Then cook them!	Jen's father doesn't dispute her position, but instead gives her an alternative—if she wants cooked carrots, she will have to cook them.
Jen: Okay. I'll eat them raw.	Jen agrees to eat raw carrots, a solution that advances her own and her father's interests.

between children and adults. In each example, the parent stands firm on his or her own interests and standards while being sensitive, whenever possible, to the interests that motivate a child's misbehavior. In so doing, parents help children advance their own motives appropriately and in ways that respect the parent's nonnegotiable interests, needs, and standards.

Table 6.7. At the Store

Conversation	Comment
Tom: I need some new sneakers. Can I have these? They are really cool.	Child expresses an interest in new shoes.
Mom: Not today Tom, I can't afford these right now. And I don't think you need new sneakers.	Mother states her position ("Not today") and her interests ("I can't afford them"; "you don't need new sneakers").
Tom: I need new sneakers for school. All the guys have new cool sneakers.	Tom explains his interests and attempts to convince his mother to buy him the shoes.
Mom: But wait. You just gave me two different reasons. On the one hand, you say that you need them for school. On the other hand, you said that you want to cool sneakers like your friends. If you need sneakers for school, it shouldn't matter which ones you choose. So which is it?	Seeing the contradiction in Tom's interests, his mother is aware that he is simply trying to get her to buy the shoes. To identify Tom's genuine interests, she calls the contradiction to his attention. If the shoes are for school, it should not matter to him which shoes he buys.
Tom: Those sneakers are really cool. What's wrong with wanting cool sneakers?	Tom expresses that his genuine interest is to have cool shoes.
Mom: There's nothing wrong in wanting cool sneakers. But they have to be paid for. I don't have the money for sneakers that you don't actually need right now. If you want the sneakers, you will have to find some other way to get them—maybe wait for your birthday.	Contrary to Tom's expectation, his mother acknowledges the legitimacy of his interest. However, she also identifies her own interests (i.e., not being able to afford shoes that are not really needed). She suggests a way that they can advance their interests.
Tom: How about if I do some work around the house to earn money for them?	Tom suggests an alternative solution that he hopes will be mutually satisfying.

(continued)

Table 6.7. Continued

Conversation	Comment
Mom: I like that idea. I'm impressed. I'll tell you what, you earn half the money, and I'll pay the rest. What do you think?	Tom's mother accepts his offer. Being impressed with his industriousness, she offers to pay half the cost of the shoes if Tom is successful. Note that Tom's mother does not offer to pay for half of the cost as a bargaining chip; instead, she offers because she is impressed with the suggestion and wants to support it. The offer to pay half is something the mother chose for herself.
Tom: Okay. But I really want them now.	Tom accepts the offer, even though he would rather have the shoes now.

Table 6.8. Attitude

Conversation	Comment
Mom: I have to get some fruit"	Child is sitting in the carriage at a supermarket. He is getting bored.
Jack: [*Loud and demanding*] BORING.	Child expresses his feeling, but in a rude and insensitive way.
Mom: You're bored. I'm sorry that you're bored. But saying "boring" is rude and disrespectful. Don't just say "boring." Tell me what would make you less bored.	Mother acknowledges Jack's boredom, but states her own interest—that he not simply blurt out "boring." Instead, she suggests a better strategy for helping Jack express his interests.
Jack: I'm bored. I don't want to go shopping anymore.	Jack expresses his interests in a less demanding and more sensitive way.
Mom: I need to buy some fruit. I shouldn't be long. What would make you less bored while I shop?	Mother expresses her interests (her need to continue shopping) but seeks to find a way to meet Jack's interest.
Jack: Can I get a coloring book?	Jack suggests a solution to his problem.
Mom: You can go look at the coloring books if you want. But be careful not to bend them. If you get bored, come and get me.	Mom rejects his solution, but suggests an alternative, which Jack accepts.

Table 6.9. Autonomy Seeking in Early Adolescence

Conversation	Comment
Mom: Ben, your room is a mess. Time to clean it up.	Mother makes a request.
Ben: [*Rudely*] It's my room. I can keep it messy if I want to.	The child's refuses, and justifies his refusal by claiming ownership and autonomy in his room.
Mom: You like having a messy room. We can discuss that. But not if you talk to me in a disrespectful way. If you want me to hear you out, you are going to have to change your tone.	The mother acknowledges Ben's stated interest, which, on the surface, seems to be a desire to keep his room messy. After acknowledging his interest, she firmly states her interests (not to be treated rudely) and states the conditions under which she will be motivated to attend to Ben's interests (he has to change his tone.)
Ben: [*Softer*] No. It's just that it's my room, and you're always on me.	Ben sees that his mother means business. Adjusting his tone slightly, he presses on.
Mom: You seem to be saying that you don't like me telling you what to do? That you want to be treated like an adult.	Picking up on "you're always on me," mother summarizes her understanding of what seems to be Ben's real interest—that he is seeking more autonomy.
Ben: Yes! I don't like it when you tell me how dirty my room is and that I have to clean it.	Ben verifies that his mother understands his interests, but he is still being a bit rude.
Mom: I see. I am happy to talk more about ways that we can give you more freedom to make decisions. But you are not free to do things that affect other people negatively. Having a messy room doesn't just affect you; it affects me, too. I have to see it or know that it's dirty. So, you are telling me that you want more freedom, I'm telling you that I have a desire to have a clean house—including your room.	In contrast to what Ben may have expected, his mother expresses approval of his desire for autonomy. In so doing, she supports his interest. However, she also asserts her interest to live in a clean house. She explains why her interest is legitimate—not to persuade Ben but to inform him of the reasons for her nonnegotiable interests. In doing this, she makes the conflict between them explicit—Ben wants more autonomy, but his mother wants a clean house.

(*continued*)

Table 6.9. Continued

Conversation	Comment
Ben: But it's my room. I get to choose whether I clean it or not.	Ben claims ownership of his room, disregarding his mother's stated interests.
Mom: Not necessarily. Your room is part of this house, which is mine—not yours. When you move out, you will be able to make your own decisions about your room.	Ben's mother expresses her position on his claim to own his room, which she disputes.
Ben: So you're telling me that you're okay giving me more freedom, except when it comes to my room.	In an attempt to defend his position, Ben notes an apparent contradiction in his mother's desire to give him more freedom.
Mom: No, I'm telling you that with freedom comes responsibility. Keeping your room dirty when it bothers me is both irresponsible and uncaring. I'm willing to give you more freedom, but only if you show that you are able to handle the responsibilities that come with it. For example, last week, I gave you the freedom to have someone other than me drive you home from soccer practice, but only if you call me first and I approve of who is driving. You get more freedom, but only if you can act responsibly.	Ben's mother refuses to be dragged into a debate about positions. Instead, she focuses on his interest to be given more autonomy and her own interest in having a clean house. She expresses the conditions under which she is willing to advance Ben's interests: he can earn his autonomy by being responsible to others. Through her words, Ben's mother teaches him the relation between the virtues of freedom and responsibility. She gives him the opportunity to act in ways that would allow Ben to see himself as both responsible and caring to others (e.g., cleaning up his room).
Mom: So, let's talk about ways that you can earn more freedom and I can have my desire for a clean house respected.	At this point, the conflict has been articulated, but not resolved. Ben's mother holds out an offer to continue the conversation, based on a clear demarcation of her interests and expectations.

MANAGE CONFLICT

To raise socially, morally, and intellectually competent children, teach them how to advance their own interests while compassionately respecting the interests of others.

Whell children get into conflicts, we often hear adults suggest solutions like "Let them work it out themselves," "They have to learn to work it out themselves," or even "That's how they learn—by working it out themselves."

Peer relationships are crucial aspects of children's development. Children learn a great deal from each other over time. As they interact, they acquire social skills, develop ways of being friends, learn academic skills, develop a sense of being accepted or rejected by others, and learn to be in social relationships. Children's interactions with their parents can prepare them for peer interactions, but parent–child interactions cannot replace peer interactions in development. If you need convincing of this point, simply ask yourself: from whom do you learn most in your life? The answer, of course, is your peers.

Despite the importance of peer interaction in children's development, is it always good to simply, "let them work it out themselves"? We do not allow children to figure out how to speak, perform daily living skills, learn mathematics, take responsibility for chores, learn to cook, play sports, or virtually any other skill entirely by themselves. Why would we think that something as complex as managing conflict—something that even adults tend to do poorly—would be something that children can teach each other?

Are there times when we should let children manage conflict on their own? Of course! But only when the resolution of those conflicts is something that is reasonable within their developmental grasp. The fact is that parents can exert a profound influence on children's social development by guiding them through the process of managing social conflicts. Situations involving social conflict have all of the ingredients for moving development forward—or derailing it. To teach children how to manage social conflict is to teach them to be competent problem solvers. Teaching children to manage conflict directly prompts development of their thinking skills, social relational skills, and emotional regulation skills.

Steps in Helping Children Manage Conflict

Although similar to the process of managing conflict between parents and children, because it involves at least three rather than two people, this process can be a bit more complex and nuanced.

Step 1: Managing Emotions

The first step to guiding children through the process of managing conflicts among themselves is the same as it is for managing conflict between parents and children: calmness first! However, when more than one child is involved, the process of modulating children's emotions becomes more difficult. Instead of managing the emotions of only two people (i.e., parent and child), the parent now must modulate the emotions of at least three people. There are three sets of interactions going on simultaneously—one between you and the first child, one between you and the second, and a third one between the two children themselves. With so much going on, the possibilities for emotional escalation are quite high.

> Seven-year-olds Todd and Ramone are playing calmly together with toy trucks. After a while, Todd begins to become bored playing trucks. He asks Ramone to play a computer game with him, but Ramone wants to continue to play trucks. As he becomes more involved with his trucks, Ramone begins to ignore Todd's requests. To get his attention, Todd takes one of Ramone's trucks. With an angry face, Ramone looks at Todd and screams, "That's my truck!" Todd replies, "It's my truck—you're just playing with it." The boys are now involved in a heated exchange.

Let's trace how Todd and Ramone's emotions changed over the course of their interaction. As shown in Figure 7.1, early in their interaction, when the boys were engaged in calm play, they were in an optimal emotional state. They were optimally stimulated—they were interested in and enjoying what they were doing; nothing was going so wrong as to cause frustration or distress. Their emotions were running neither too high nor too low. As Todd became bored; he began to experience a state of underactivation. He no longer found the trucks interesting and stimulating. As a result, he began to look for a new activity that would be optimally stimulating for him. Unfortunately for Todd, Ramone was happy to continue to play with the trucks. This is where the conflict between the boys actually begins—several moments before Todd seizes one of Ramone's trucks.

When Todd takes Ramone's truck (indicated at the X in Figure 7.1), Ramone's emotions immediate escalate. He is now in a state of overactivation. His emotionally charged response "That's my truck—give it back!" activate's Todd's emotional state. He shifts abruptly from an underactivated emotional state to an overactivated one! Now there are two boys in the

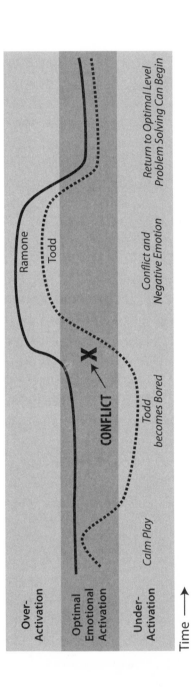

Over-
Activation

Optimal
Emotional
Activation

Under-
Activation

Ramone

Todd

CONFLICT

Todd
becomes Bored

Calm Play

Conflict and
Negative Emotion

Return to Optimal Level
Problem Solving Can Begin

Time ——→

Figure 7.1. Optimal Emotional Activation

overactivated zone. Conflicts are not managed well when emotions are running high.

The parent enters a situation with two boys whose emotions are escalating. How is it likely that the parent will respond? Emotions are contagious. When we encounter someone else who is distressed, frustrated, or angry, our own emotional state begins to escalate. When greeted with two fighting children, even the calmest parent's emotions tend to escalate. In such situations, just like children, parents struggle to keep their emotions in a state of optimal activation. This is why managing emotions is such an important aspect of mediating conflicts between people.

To manage children's emotions, focus on their concerns. It is typically easier to manage emotions in situations that involve a parent and a child. When engaging a child one on one, the parent and the child can attend directly to each other. As a result, it is easier to exert control over the events that bring about emotions in children. In conflicts that involve two or more children, the situation is more complex. In most such situations, something must be done to bring children's emotions under control. The same strategies described earlier for managing emotions in conflicts between parents and children can be used to in situations involving conflict between children (e.g., waiting until everyone is calm, taking a break). However, when the stakes are higher, parents will often find that they need more nuanced ways to manage children's emotions.

When we think about calming our emotions, we often get into a trap. On the one hand, we know that emotions are something that happen to us; they are not something that we can simply make happen at will. On the other hand, when we are experiencing an emotion, we are able to exert some degree of control over it. We can inhibit or suppress the feeling, vent it, take a series of deep breaths, and so on. Using such strategies can help us calm ourselves. With a few exceptions, focusing on the feeling itself is probably not the best way to manage emotions. Such strategies tend to work only in the short term and have a limited effect. For example, taking a series of deep breaths can help us calm ourselves when we are angry, distressed, or even overjoyed. However, once calm, if we focus again on the events that brought about these emotions, our feelings tend to recur.

Emotions are reactions to the fate of our interests and concerns. We feel happy when we get what we want, angry when things are different from the way they should be, sad when we irrevocably lose something that we wanted, afraid when we believe that danger is looming, and so forth. If this is so, then the most direct way of modifying emotions—whether they exist in adults or children—is to focus on the concerns that are involved in generating our emotions. That is, instead of trying to control the feeling of an emotion, it is better to tend to the interests, motives, and concerns that produce them. Sandy is angry because Tom took a wanted toy; Sandy wants her toy back. Sarah's feelings are hurt because David called her a name; she wants an apology. Rick feels sad because Tony broke his toy; he wants his toy fixed. Wendy is afraid that Dan won't play fair; she wants to be reassured that he will.

In situations that involve conflict between children, emotions run high. Typically, each child involved in a conflict may feel wronged by the other. Children are frustrated; they want their concerns to be heard and addressed. There are at least two issues going on in any conflict. The first is the particular issue at hand—the specific disagreement or dispute that calls for resolution. The second is the desire to be heard, acknowledged, and respected.

A large part of the emotional burden of conflict is the fear that one's concerns will not be acknowledged. In such situations, parents can help children calm their emotional states simply by reassuring them that their concerns will be heard and addressed. Such reassurance can have an immediate effect. By removing a large part of the emotional burden of the conflict, children can begin to calm themselves and focus on the problem at hand. This is especially true if parents have established a history of acknowledging their children's interests and giving the opportunity to express their feelings and concerns.

In conflicts involving emotional distress, parents can adopt some version of the following:

1. Separate the children from the conflict. Depending on the intensity of the conflict, this step can range from simply having children stop interacting to having them spend time in separate physical locations where they can have a break from seeing or hearing each other. This gives them an opportunity to begin to calm themselves. Depending on the conflict, a parent can say:
   - "I see that you are not playing well together right now. Let's stop playing and talk this out."
   - "We don't raise our voices when we have a problem. Stop fighting this moment. Let's talk this out. Boys, lets each sit down and calm ourselves. Then we can talk."
   - "I can see that both of you are very upset. I don't want you to talk to each other right now. Todd, please go into the kitchen so that you can calm down. Ramone, please sit on the couch."

2. Reassure children that their concerns will be addressed. Ensure that each child knows he will have the opportunity to express his concerns and have them addressed. If you have a sense of what the child's interests actually are in the situation, it is often helpful to state them as you him. A parent might say:
   - "Have a seat, boys. Don't worry, we'll talk this through together."
   - "Don't worry boys, you'll each get a chance to say what you want."
   - "Ramone, I know you want your toy back. We'll deal with that. Todd, I'm not sure what you want, but you can talk about it in a minute."

3. Use additional means to help children calm their emotional states. Parents can use any number of additional strategies to help calm their children. For example, they can direct children to take a series of deep breaths or attend mindfully to their breathing. Some children are able to calm themselves more quickly if they know that being calm is a prerequisite for being able to voice their concerns. A parent can say, "Okay, it's time to calm down. When you are calm, we can begin our discussion," or "You won't be able to explain what you want until you are totally calm," or something similar.

Figure 7.2 shows how focusing on a child's concerns in a conflict can help him or her modulate emotions. During interpersonal conflict (1), children become confused and emotionally overloaded. Because so much is going on at once, they are likely to be experiencing many different thoughts. Since they are emotionally upset, they may have difficulty focusing and expressing their thoughts. They are often distracted and over-

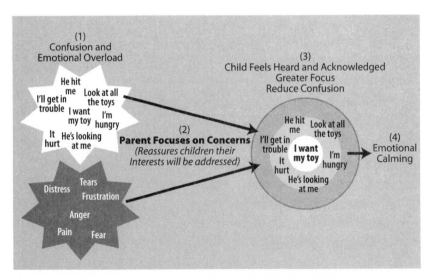

Figure 7.2. Focusing on Concerns to Modulate Emotion

whelmed by the situation. Furthermore, in a conflict, neither child can be confident that she will be able to advance her interests and get what she wants. Children are typically worried that their views will not be heard.

Consider what happens when a parent focuses his intervention on children's concerns (2) that generate children's feelings rather than on the feelings themselves. A parent might say to a child, "I see that Todd took your toy and you want it back. We are going to deal with that." At this point, the parent's statements operate as a kind of "zoom lens" (3) for the child. The parent directs the child's attention to his primary concerns—something that the confused and overwhelmed child may not be able to do for himself. In so doing, the parent simultaneously helps children focus their attention, cuts out distracting thoughts, reassures children that the parent understands and wants to help address their concerns. The effect of zooming in on the child's core concerns focuses his attention to what is most important—"I want my toy"—and relegates other concerns to the periphery. This reduces the emotional burden on the child, leading to an increased capacity for emotional calming (4).

Giving children the opportunity to have their concerns addressed is not the same as ensuring that a child will have her interests met. To determine whether and how it is possible to meet each child's interests and concerns in an appropriate way is the purpose of the problem-solving discussion.

Step 2: Set the Ground Rules

After children have managed to calm themselves, it's time to bring them together and set the ground rules for shared problem solving. These should typically be short and clearly articulated, especially for young children. Families can set any ground rules they wish. A parent may say something like the following:

Okay, we're ready to talk. Now we have to have some ground rules. These are rules that you both have to follow. First, when Todd is talking, Ramone and I have to listen carefully. When Ramone is talking, Todd and I have to listen carefully. No interrupting. Okay? Do you understand?

We have to remain calm throughout our discussion, or else we are going to have to stop. If that happens, you will have to calm yourself for us to begin again. You won't be able to say what you want until you are calm.

Todd, after Ramone tells us how he felt, I want to make sure that you understand what he is saying. So, I'm going to ask you some questions about what he said. So listen carefully. You'll have a chance to say how you felt later. Okay? [Repeat for other child.]

Step 3: Help Children Identify and Understanding Each Other's Interests and Feelings

Now it is time to lead the problem-solving discussion. The goals of the discussion are to help each person understand each other's interests (including those of the parent) in an attempt to develop ways to resolve the conflict between the children for mutual gain. Some important steps follow. There are many ways to lead a problem-solving discussion; there is no single procedure that can apply to all situations. Parents should rely on their intuition, their knowledge of the situation, and their sense of what is best. Against this backdrop, here are some guidelines and suggestions.

1. Help each child describe his perspective on what happened. Children will want to state their view of what happened. This can sometimes be difficult for the other child, who will often want to state his side of the story immediately. The trick is to help the first child state his case without causing undue upset in

the other. The role of the parent is not necessarily to gain information to determine who is right. It is more important to gain information so that each child can understand the other's views and work toward a mutually beneficial solution.

PARENT: Ramone, you go first. First, in your own words, tell me what happened. Todd, remember, just listen. Don't interrupt—even if you don't agree with him. You'll have a chance to say what you think happened later. Okay? Go ahead Ramone, what happened?

RAMONE: We were playing trucks together. And for no reason he just grabbed my yellow truck from my hand. I told him to please give it back, but he wouldn't.

PARENT: What did you say to Todd just before he took it?

RAMONE: Nothing. We weren't talking then.

PARENT: [*After child completes description*] Thanks, Ramone. Now, let me see if I have this straight? [*Parent summarizes child's description.*] Is that right? Did I get anything wrong? Is there something you want to add?

2. Help each child articulate his genuine interests (wants, desires, goals) in the situation. In any conflict involving other children, kids will usually have two types of interests: the "official" ones that they want you to hear, and the real, "unofficial" ones. The more genuine and unofficial interests are the most important. At first, children often may not know their real interests in a given situation. They may be reluctant to reveal their genuine interests out a fear of parental disapproval. If, however, a parent genuinely wishes to help a child advance his legitimate genuine interests in appropriate way, it is necessary not only to help children articulate those interests but to accept them as well. It is not necessary to approve of an interest in order to

accept it. Accepting a child's interest requires that we understand and empathize with it, even when we do not approve of it. If children come to learn that their interests will be accepted, they will feel safe enough to express them. If children come to see that parents are genuinely invested in helping children advance those interests in effective ways, they will be more likely to accept and even seek out parental guidance.

PARENT: [*Using a nonjudgmental tone*] Okay, Todd, why did you take the toy from Ramone? What was it that you wanted?

TODD: I wanted Ramone to play with me.

PARENT: You grabbed the truck because you wanted him to play with you?

TODD: Yes.

PARENT: Why did you think that would make him want to play with you?

TODD: I don't know. I just wanted him to play.

3. Help each child explain, using emotion words, how he feels in the situation and why. By encouraging children to use emotion words, parents can help them learn to identify their emotional states. Young children will typically use simple words like *mad*, *sad*, *scared*, *yucky*, or *happy*. Parents can help older children learn to use more precise emotion words, such as *annoyed*, *ashamed*, *bored*, *embarrassed*, *frustrated*, *guilty*, *hurt*, *jealous*, *surprised*,. Using emotion words also helps the child's partner more easily understand and talk about how the questioned child felt.

PARENT: How did you feel when Todd grabbed the yellow truck?

RAMONE: Mad! Like I wanted to punch him!

PARENT: Why did you feel so mad?

RAMONE: Because he grabbed it from me.

4. Help each child summarize (a) what his partner wanted in the situation, (b) how his partner felt, and (c) why. This step is important for helping each child feel heard and understood by the other child. In addition, having the listener describe the speaker's point of view forces the listener to attend closely to what the speaker is saying. It is often difficult for children (of any age) to describe the feelings of the speaker. This is to be expected. When this occurs, it is often helpful for the parent to provide firm but gentle guidance and prompting. When the child is able to respond appropriately, it is helpful for parents to comment on the virtue of the child's behavior (e.g., that was hard for you; it took a lot of courage for you to say that; you seemed genuine — that was a very caring way to say it).

PARENT: Okay, Todd, how did Ramone feel in this situation? How did he say he felt?

TODD: I didn't want to keep playing trucks! We were playing a long time.

PARENT: Yes, Todd, I understand. You will get to tell me more later. Right now, I just want you to tell me how Ramone felt.

TODD: I don't know.

PARENT: You don't know? I think you heard him. Do you want me to ask him to say it again? Or can you tell me?

TODD: Mad.

PARENT: Yes, good for you. You were listening. Why did he feel that way?

TODD: I took it.

PARENT: You took what?

TODD: The stupid truck.

PARENT: Thanks, Todd. That was hard for you to say, but you did it anyway. Good job.

5. Explain the parent's rules, standards, and expectations in the situation. After both children have had the opportunity to express their version of the event, their interests, and their feelings, it is important for the parent to express her views as well. This can be done simply by describing the parent's rules and expectations for the situation and by providing an explanation of the reasoning behind those rules (see Key 3).

    PARENT: Todd, it is perfectly okay for you to want to play a different game. But you can't get Ramone's attention by grabbing his toys. We don't grab from each other. First, if you want something, you ask. It's Ramone's decision whether he wants to give you the toy. But in this situation, you seem to be frustrated that Ramone wanted to continue to play with trucks when you wanted to play something else. Grabbing the toy from Ramone isn't going to make him want to play with you! It will make him not want to play with you . . .

Step 4: Brainstorm and Select Solutions for Mutual Gain

1. Help the children propose different ways to solve the problem between them without violating the parent's rules and expectations. This is one of the most important and perhaps difficult steps in the process. The goal of the parent is to help the children propose solutions to their conflict that are sensitive to each person's interests—including the parents. This can be difficult for children to do. It requires them to keep both their own and their partner's interests in mind while at the same time thinking of possible solutions to the conflict. As a result, the parent's guidance is especially important in this step. The goal of the parent is to guide the children through the process of inventing possible win-win solutions.

Optimally, it is best if the solutions come from the children themselves. Although this is possible, as problems become more difficult, it become harder for children to think of solutions When this happens, before nominating suggestions themselves (a temptation that can be very difficult to inhibit), parents may consider the strategy of asking guiding questions. Guiding questions direct a child's attention toward some possible solution without actually suggesting the solution. This has the effect of requiring a degree of inventive thought on the part of the child, even if the parent is supporting and guiding the child's thinking.

PARENT: Okay, Todd, if I've got this right, you were kind of bored playing with the trucks. You wanted to play something else but Ramone didn't want to. Is that right? [*Yes.*] Ramone, you wanted to keep on playing with the trucks, but you said that you didn't really mind playing something else, right? [*Yeah, after a while. I wanted to keep playing more. But it would be okay to play something else after a while.*] Okay. So Todd wants to play something else, and Ramone wants to play trucks for a while. What can we do to fix this?

RAMONE: [*Playfully, in exaggerated tone*] You could *ask* me and not just *grab* stuff.

TODD: [*In a similar tone*] You can *do something I want* and not just *ignore me*.

PARENT: So, Todd, what do you think of Ramone's suggestion that you might try asking?

TODD: I can do that. But I did ask, and he just ignored me.

PARENT: Ramone, what did you say to Todd after he said he wanted to play something else?

RAMONE: Uh, nothing.

PARENT: How do you think Todd felt when you didn't say anything?

RAMONE: Frustrated?

PARENT: Todd, how did you feel when he didn't respond to you?

TODD: Yeah, frustrated. Like you just ignored me.

PARENT: Todd, what could have done when you felt ignored by Ramone?

TODD: I could have said, "don't ignore me."

PARENT: It might be better to say, "I feel like you're ignoring me." If you say, "Don't ignore me," Ramone might feel like you're telling him what to do. If you say "I feel like," Ramone might learn something about how you felt when he didn't respond.

TODD: I feel like you're ignoring me, Ramone!

PARENT: What can you say to Todd to make him feel like you weren't ignoring him?

RAMONE: I could say, "I want to keep playing trucks for now. But maybe we can play something else in a few minutes."

2. Decide together on a solution for mutual gain and put it into action. After some possible solutions have been proposed, it is time to select a solution to the problem that maximizes the gain for both children, while simultaneously honoring the parent's rules and expectations. Again, for more difficult problems, this often requires guidance on the part of the parent to remind children of the various possible solutions that were proposed (including those proposed by the parent), as well as the possible consequences of those solutions. In the end, each person should agree on the solution and understand the possible benefits for each child. Few solutions to conflicts between people are perfect. Virtually all solutions, even when they result in mutual gain, may contain some downside or risk.

Whenever possible, children should be aware of these downsides.

PARENT: So what do we have here? Todd, there were some things that you said you could do to get Ramone's attention besides grabbing his toys. Ramone, you said that there were some things you could do besides simply ignoring Todd because you didn't want to play something else. What were they? Can we think of a way that both of you can get what you want, but without either grabbing or ignoring?

TODD: I said I could ask Ramone if he wanted to play something else. Which I did. But when he ignored me, I could say, "Please don't ignore me."

PARENT: Todd, that's great. What might Ramone do if you said that?

TODD: He could keep ignoring me, or he could say "Yes, I'll play," or "Wait," or something.

PARENT: What if he kept ignoring you?

TODD: I could say, "Please don't ignore me" again, or I can get you.

PARENT: Good. That's an example of standing up for yourself even if the other person doesn't act the way that you expect. This is called "taking the high road." Now Ramone, what did you say you could do instead of ignoring Todd if you didn't want to play?

RAMONE: I could say, "I wanna keep playing trucks, but maybe later."

PARENT: Good. Do these seem like good ideas? Does this seem like something you can do?

BOYS: Yes.

PARENT: Okay, then, let's practice . . .

3. Help children find ways to repair the interaction between them by apologizing or otherwise acknowledg-

ing the other person's perspective. Genuine apologies and acknowledgments are best. After solutions to a conflict have been formulated, it is helpful to take the final steps to repair any hurt feelings that remain after the encounter. Children can be encouraged to apologize, state what they learned from the other person, state how they feel toward the other person, shake hands, or engage in similar reparative interactions.

PARENT: So Todd, now you see that there are things you can do other than grabbing to get Ramone's attention. How do you feel about grabbing Ramone's toy?

TODD: Not good.

PARENT: What do you mean not good? Do you feel sad, angry, sorry? What words would you use?

TODD: I feel bad.

PARENT: You feel bad. Well, I can understand that. I would feel kind of bad if I knew that I did something to upset a friend. So, if you feel bad, what can you do about it?

TODD: Say I'm sorry? Sorry, Ramone.

PARENT: That's good. What do you think, Ramone? Do you think you can accept Todd's apology? Accepting an apology means that you believe that Todd is really sorry and that you agree to forgive him. What do you say?

RAMONE: Okay. I forgive you, Todd.

PARENT: Todd? Ramone just forgave you. Is there something you think you should say to him?

TODD: Thank you, Ramone.

Optimally, to repair a difficult interaction, it is important that both children understand each other's interests, positions, and feelings and that any apologies and acts of forgiveness are genuine. This is not always possible. For example, what might happen if

Ramone genuinely feels as though he has done nothing wrong?

PARENT: And what about you, Ramone? Do you feel badly about anything that you might have one?

RAMONE: No.

PARENT: No? Really? But why did Todd feel as though he had to grab the toys?

RAMONE: Oh yeah, I was ignoring him. [*Weakly*] Sorry, Todd.

PARENT: Remember, if you are sorry, that means that you think you did something wrong and that you agree to try your hardest not to do it again. Is that what you are saying?

RAMONE: Kind of.

PARENT: What do you mean, "kind of"? You have to be honest, Ramone. When you say "kind of," does that mean that you don't think you did anything that you have to apologize for?

RAMONE: Well, I wanted to keep on playing, and I told him that, and he didn't listen. So I don't really think I did something wrong by ignoring him.

PARENT: I see. So, you thought you didn't have any other choice other than to ignore Todd.

RAMONE: Yeah.

PARENT: What do you think, Todd? Can you understand how Ramone might think that the only thing he could have done was to ignore you?

TODD: Yeah.

PARENT: How can we solve this problem? If Ramone doesn't want to play, and he says so, do you think it's okay for you to keep on asking him?

TODD: No.

PARENT: Then what do you think should happen when

you ask Ramone to play something different and he says "no."

TODD: Maybe ask him later?

PARENT: That sounds like a good start.

In this example, Ramone did not feel as though he did something that warranted an apology. If a child feels this way, it is helpful to explore why. It is generally not helpful to lecture the child on what he did wrong and demand an apology. Instead, by focusing on the child's genuine interests and concerns, it is often possible to help him articulate why he feels as though he didn't do anything wrong. When this happens, children will feel heard and respected. When they feel less defensive, they may be able to identify what they did that warrants an apology (if anything). Alternatively, they may express their interests clearly and convincingly, as occurred in the example with Ramone.

Task 7.1. Teaching Children to Manage Conflicts

Teaching children to manage conflicts that occur between them is no easy task! There is no single procedure, set of steps, or script for doing so. In fact, in everyday life, children (and adults) will rarely if ever follow a script that you might plan beforehand. Life is too messy. Nonetheless, it helps to have a sense of the various things that a parent can try to do when helping children resolve their conflicts. In the situation described in the diagram below, Sandy and Tyler were playing on the computer together. Tyler got bored and wanted to do something else. He asked Sandy if they could play something different, but Sandy ignored him. As a result, Tyler shut off the computer that Sandy was using and Sandy called Tyler a "loser."

When teaching children to manage conflicts, it is helpful to guide them through a series of loosely organized steps. First, after ensuring that everyone is calm, you can begin the process by asking each child to describe what happened. A parent can use the blank diagram to guide children through the conflict management process. The parent begins by assigning each child in the conflict to one of the characters shown in the diagram. After flipping a coin or using some similar procedure to decide which child will be questioned first, the parent asks each individual child to describe his or her own behaviors, thoughts and feelings in the situation. (In this procedure, there is no reason to ask each child to describe what the other child did; children will not be able to stop themselves from describing the other child's behavior during questioning—especially when asked question 2). For each child independently, the parent asks:

1. What did you do in this situation?
2. Why did you do that? What is it that you wanted? What were you trying to get by doing that?
3. How did you feel when that happened?

Having asked these questions, the parent then helps each child understand the interests and feelings that motivated the behaviors involved in the conflict. This typically will require that parents help children work through defensive feelings as they try to under-

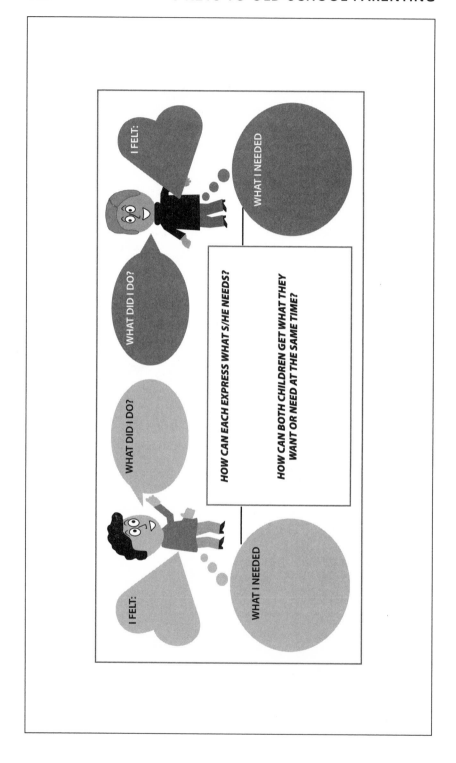

stand why the other child acted and felt the way he or she did. However, *once children are able to describe with understanding how the other child's interests, feelings and behaviors,* the pair will be ready for the problem-solving questions:

4. How can you work together so that each of you gets you want? How can each of you show that you care about what the other wants and feels?

The results of children's (guided) brainstorming can be written in the space provided. It is possible to record many different ways of solving the problem between the two children, or simply recording the best solution to the problem. The diagram is meant to function as a tool to help parents through the process. It can be used in any way that is helpful to parents and children.

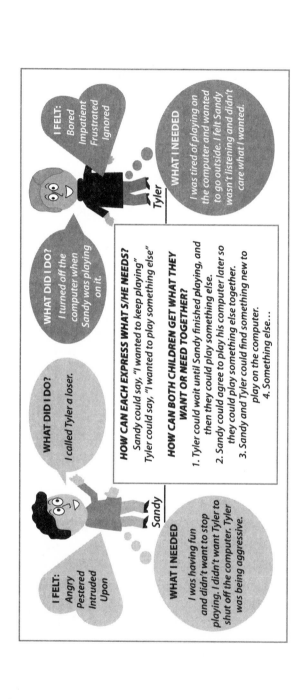

KEY 8

COMMUNICATE EFFECTIVELY

You can hear a lot just by listening.

$$=======$$

In any attempt to resolve conflict between two people, two tools stand out as most effective. They are (1) empathetic listening and (2) asserting interests. These tools are relevant not only for conflicts that occur between parents and children, but any form of conflict, including conflicts between adults, conflicts within a marriage, conflicts in the workplace, and even conflicts between children.

The Listener's Job: Empathetic Listening

Let's start with empathetic listening.

> *You've had a hard day and you are exhausted. You are looking forward to relaxing after work. No cooking tonight. You want to go out to dinner, or at least order pizza. You come home and begin to tell your spouse about your day. However, your spouse cuts you off when you say that you want to go out for dinner: "We really can't afford to go out to dinner so often. We should stay home."*

How do you feel? If you are like most people, you probably feel unheard, unacknowledged, not listened to, angry, and perhaps a bit hurt. Why? Because your spouse did not want to go out to dinner? Probably not. It's because the thing you wanted most in this situation was for your feelings to be acknowledged. Here you are, frustrated and exhausted from a hard day's work, and your spouse has effectively ignored your feelings.

The desire to be heard — to have one's feelings understood and acknowledged — is not confined to situations like this. It is one of our strongest desires. This is especially true when it comes to situations that involve conflict between people. Here, rather than trying to understand one another, it is very easy to get into a cycle of anger.

SALLY: Mom, can I stay up an hour later tonight?

MOM: Sally, you know you are supposed to go to bed at 8:30.

SALLY: But Mom, I'm nine years old. You're treating me like a little kid.

MOM: No, I'm not — I just want you to have enough sleep.

SALLY: No you don't. If you didn't think I was a kid, you'd let me stay up later.

MOM: Don't you talk to me that way! If you don't want to be treated like a little kid, then you should stop acting like one.

Neither Sally nor her mother is feeling particularly understood or heard in this situation. Neither is making a genuine attempt to acknowledge the other person's feelings. Instead, their conversation descends into blame and defensiveness. "You know you are supposed to go to bed by . . . ", "You don't trust me," "I do so . . .", and so forth.

Empathetic listening occurs when one person temporarily puts aside his or her interests and attempts to understand what another person is thinking and feeling. In empathetic listening, one decides to stop, listen, attend, and care. One devotes all his or her attention to the other person in an attempt to see the world from that person's perspective. The empathetic listener does not interrupt and does not attempt to counter or respond to the other person's statements. His or her goal is simply to understand the other person empathetically. The empathetic listener does not just want to understand the other person's thoughts and feelings; optimally, the listener's goal is to feel empathy for the other person—to feel what they feel as they take the other person's perspective.

It is helpful to break empathetic listening down into a series of parts or steps. The most important part of being an empathetic listener is simply to care. It means putting yourself in the shoes of your child and trying to experience a situation the way she does. Beyond that, to be a good empathetic listener, consider doing the following:

1. Stop what you are doing. Devote all of your attention to the speaker. Try to put yourself in the position of the speaker.
2. Listen actively so that you understand and can remember what the speaker is saying. Look at the person; nod your head to indicate you understand; make comments that encourage the speaker to continue to express him- or herself.
3. When the speaker is done speaking, summarize or reflect back what the person has said in your own words. Be complete. After you summarize what the speaker has said, ask him or her, "Is that what you are saying?" or "Do I understand you correctly?" or something similar.
4. When the speaker indicates that you understand and empathize with what he or she is saying, comment on what you believe the listener must be feeling. You can say, "It sounds as if you were really hurt when he said that to you," "That's an awful way to feel," or "It seems important to you to feel like a big kid. I wouldn't want to feel like a little kid either if I were you."

Here is an example of empathetic listening.

SALLY: Mom, I'd like to change my bedtime. I'd like to be able to stay up later.

MOM: You want to be able to stay up past 8:30?

SALLY: Yeah. Can I stay up until 9:30?

MOM: What's going on? Why do you want your bedtime to be 9:30?

SALLY: I don't know. Jackie, Tom, and Alice all get to go to bed at 9:30. I should be able to go to bed at 9:30, too.

MOM: Uh huh. You want to stay up as late as your friends do.

SALLY: Yeah. I think I'm old enough to stay up later.

MOM: I see. I want you to be able to stay up as late as your friends. Tell me, why do you feel as though you have to go to be at the same time as Jackie, Alice, and Tom?

SALLY: All the kids stay up later. It makes me feel like a little kid that I can't stay up later. They'll make fun of me.

MOM: It sounds like you are kind of saying staying up later would make you feel more in step with your friends. Is that right?

SALLY: Well, yeah! It's kind of embarrassing to be the only one that has to go to bed early.

MOM: You feel embarrassed to tell them what time you have to go to bed, huh? That's a crummy way to feel.

What has happened in this situation? When Sally speaks, Mom invites her to engage in further conversation. She may do this by asking open-ended questions ("What's going on? Why do you want to stay up until 9:30?"). More often, Mom simply expresses interest ("Uh huh," "I see"), reflects back or summarizes ("You want to be able to stay up as late as your friends"), or extends or clarifies what Sally said ("It sounds like you are kind of saying staying up later would make you feel more in step with your friends").

More important, note what Mom has *not* done. She has not said "yes" or "no" yet to Sally's request. She has not interrupted her daughter. She has not become angry. Even is she disagrees with something Sally might have said (e.g., "All the kids are staying up late"), Mom has not become defensive (e.g., she doesn't say, "Well you're not all kids" or something similar). She has not blamed Sally for anything. She has not called Sally any names.

Empathetic listening is not always an easy thing to do. It's difficult to put one's reactions aside and imagine the position of another person—especially when what the other person is saying is at odds with what we want. However, one person does not have to agree with another person to engage in empathetic listening. Several things happen when one person listens empathetically to another:

1. The listener is able to learn things about what the speaker is actually thinking and feeling that would be simply impossible otherwise.
2. By understanding how the other person truly thinks and feels, the listener gains a sense of compassion for the speaker.
3. As a result, the listener becomes less defensive.
4. The speaker feels heard. The speaker feels that his or her feelings have been understood and acknowledged.
5. The speaker feels that the listener cares about him or her and wants what is best for the speaker.
6. Because the listener feels heard and acknowledged, he or she is more likely to listen to what the listener has to say when it is the listener's turn to speak.

As a result of Mom's empathetic listening, Sally felt safe enough to explain what wants and how she feels. Mom has gained some very valuable information. Most important, Sally feels heard and understood. Imagine how it must feel to Sally to know that he mother not only understands her embarrassment in front of her friends but also empathizes with it!

Some parents feel uncomfortable with some of these techniques. For example, some parents feel as though they are not acting naturally when they repeat back what a child has said. It feels odd or unlike everyday ways of speaking. This is understandable. If such ways of speaking are new, they are likely to feel uncomfortable. However, many parents are surprised when such ways of speaking work and make children feel more comfortable speaking. When this happens, what at first seemed uncomfortable becomes a part of everyday conversation.

The key to effectively summarizing and reflecting back what your child has said is to be genuinely interested in communicating to your child that you fully understand and care about what she is saying. A parent who tries to memorize and repeats back what a child says without genuinely understanding or trying to empathize is not engaging in empathetic listening. Such a person is acting more like a robot. When this happens, the child will become aware that the parent is not being genuine. Both the parent and the child will feel uncomfortable and awkward. However, a parent cannot go wrong if he is genuinely sincere in his attempt to empathize with a child. If you are being genuine, your child will feel it.

Task 8.1. Active Listening can be Hard—Write it Down!

Active listening can be a challenge—for both children and parents. This is especially so when emotions run high. The biggest obstacle to empathetic listening is the desire to express one's own slights and hurts when one's partner is expressing theirs. Furthermore, under the best of circumstances, it's hard to remember enough of what a child says to summarize and acknowledge his or her version of an event. Practice helps. Consider actually writing down what a child says when he or she describes an event—whether or not it involves conflict. Writing down what a child says can help you to see how much we tend to miss even when try hard to listen to each other carefully and sympathetically.

People can and do talk this way. When they are able to do so, conversations go much more smoothly. Of course, this example of conflict is not yet resolved. Mom has very ably helped Sally to express her true interests. Now it's time for Mom to express her interests and legitimate prerogatives to Sally.

The Speaker's Job: Sensitive Self-Assertion

In the example of Sally and her mother, Mom was able to help Sally identify her genuine interests. Sally says that she wants to stay up later; that is her position. Her mother was able to help Sally articulate the more important issue: she wants to feel more grown up and independent. Now that Sally's mother has listened and heard these genuine interests, it's time for Mom to assert *her* interests.

In most everyday conflicts, people tend to think that getting the opportunity to speak is an occasion to advance one's position on an issue. It gives the person the opportunity to express what he thinks is right and what the other person has done wrong. Whenever there is heated conflict between two children, "you" is likely to be the most frequently heard word. That is because children are busy blaming each other for what they think went wrong. Between parents and children, it is usually the parent who is doing the blaming (usually, of course, with some justification). When this happens, the opportunity for meaningful conflict resolution has all but passed.

For effective conflict management to take place, it is necessary to separate the person from the problem. Problem solving tends to go wrong when people fail to separate the people from the problem. We confuse the people with the problem when we blame others for the problem, attack the other person, or insult or devalue the other party in some way. Conversely, people and problems are not separated if we find ourselves taking the problem personally, when we fail to separate our interests from our positions, or if we feel we are being blamed or insulted.

Whenever this happens, it's time to pull back and reflect on what we are doing.

In a conflict, the child is not the problem; the problem is the problem. Win-win solutions are able to meet the genuine and legitimate interests of parents and children. The issue is how to reconcile each person's genuine interests. If this is so, when a person gains the opportunity to speak, his job becomes that of stating his interests, wants, goals, and concerns so that they can be part of a problem-solving conversation. Stating interests has nothing to do with assigning blame to others. When we state our interests, we are not talking about the other person. Instead, we are talking about ourselves. Stating interests does not involve pointing fingers at others. We merely explain what is inside of us—what we want, what we feel, what we believe.

The Concept of an I-Statement

Stating our interests seems like it should be simple. However, it can sometimes be a challenge. The trick to asserting one's interests is to understand that doing so is not the same as blaming, attacking, instructing, demanding, reprimanding, or the like. Asserting one's interests means talking about one's own desires, values, goals, needs, and standards. It means digging deep and identify what it is that you, as a parent, really want and why.

When stating one's interests, one is talking primarily about one's self. This is best done by using what is often called an "I-statement". An I-statement is a statement is about one's self. It reveals one's genuine thoughts, feelings, concerns, and standards. It is called an I-statement because it most often begins with the word *I*. I-statements begin with phrases like:

- I feel . . .
- I think . . .
- I want . . .
- When you say that, I feel . . .
- That is acceptable to me . . .

- That is not acceptable to me . . .
- My interests here are . . .
- What I'm concerned about is . . .

I-statements contrast with "you-statements," which are statements that characterize, blame, or demean the other person.

- You are a bad boy.
- You never do what I ask.
- I've told you over and over . . .
- You are always procrastinating!

Such statements often cause defensiveness in the person hearing them. Even though such statements are not effective in the long run, parents can seem to get away with using them with young children. This is merely because parents have more power than their young children. As children get older, they will be more able to assert their own power. When this happens, the result is a power struggle. A power struggle is the least effective way to manage conflict between parents and children (or anyone else for that matter). The winner will always be the more powerful; when that happens, everyone loses.

I-statements allow a person to state his or her own interests without blaming or demeaning the other person (whether that person is a parent or child). I-statements identify one's interests as something that must be acknowledged, attended to, respected, and met in any given collaborative exchange. Using I-statements to assert your interests has considerable power, especially when your child feels as though you are motivated to hear and even meet his or her legitimate interests.

Let's put this into action by continuing the dialogue between Sally and her mother.

Mom: So, I understand that you want to be able to stay up until 9:30. You want to be a big kid, and staying up later is something that big kids do. That makes a lot of sense. I can see that it can be embarrassing if your friends find out that you go to bed an hour earlier than they do. I would probably feel the same way if I were in your shoes.

SALLY: Yeah, it makes me feel like a little kid. So, I can stay up?

MOM: Well, let's talk this through. I like the fact that you are wanting to be a big kid. That means you want more independence and more responsibility. I'm worried, however, about your sleep. Last week, we got out of the house late on Monday and Thursday. It's been hard for you to get up in the morning. And sometimes, when you get home from school you are very tired. It's not your bedtime that I'm worried about—I am most concerned about you getting enough sleep.

SALLY: You're treating me like a little kid.

MOM: You think that if I don't let you stay up late, I'm treating you like a baby.

SALLY: Yeah! My friends get to stay up.

MOM: It's important to you that I don't treat you like a baby.

SALLY: Of course it is. I'm not a kid, you know.

MOM: Okay, I don't want to make you feel like a little kid. But I want you to be fully rested in the morning. I want us to be able to get out of the house on time in the morning, and without you being sleepy. How can we solve this problem?

In this interaction, Sally's mother has shown that she understand her daughter's interests (not being treated like a little kid). She does this by summarizing and expressing care about Sally's stated interests:

- "I can see that it can be embarrassing if your friends find out that you go to bed an hour earlier than they do. I would probably feel the same way as you if I were in your shoes."
- "You think that if I don't let you stay up late, I'm treating you like a baby."
- "I don't want to make you feel like a little kid."

Sally's mother, however, has also expressed her own interests (i.e., wanting Sally to get enough rest). In so doing she has not blamed Sally or made negative comments about her friends or their parents. Instead, she used a series of I-statements to communicate her own interests:

- "It's not your bedtime that I'm worried about—I am most concerned about you getting enough sleep."
- "I want you to be fully rested in the morning."
- "I want us to be able to get out of the house on time in the morning, and without you being sleepy."

Sally's mother has communicated respect for Sally's interests while also insisting on respect for her own interests. The problem—which may or may not be solvable—is one of finding a way to advance Sally's interest of not feeling like a little kid while advancing her mother's nonnegotiable interest of having Sally get sufficient rest. By using I-statements to communicate her interests, Mom does nothing to diminish the importance of Sally's interests. An I-statement is simply a statement of what Sally's mother wants. If there are ways to meet her interests, Sally's mother's interests need not clash with Sally's.

Are You-Statements Always Damaging?

In parent–child interactions, it is probably not possible to do away with you-statements entirely. That is because the relationship between parent and child is not equal; parents have legitimate authority over their children. Part of that authority involves identifying when children have acted inappropriately and stating more appropriate modes of behavior. As a result, it is often necessary and even desirable to use you-statements, such as:

- "You just hit your sister; that is unacceptable."
- "When you came home late, you broke a family rule."
- "It's time for you to do your homework."

Table 8.1. You-Statements

Characterizing or Demeaning Language	Descriptive Language
"You are always procrastinating!"	"You haven't done your homework yet."
"You are a mean brother! You are horrible to your sister!"	"You made your sister cry when you told her that you hate her."
"You are too immature to stay out late."	"Last week, you said you would come home at 10, but you stayed out until 11. I need to be able to trust that you will keep your word before I allow you to stay out later."
"You lied when you said you'd get off the computer at 1 pm."	"I asked you to get off of the computer at 1:00, but now it's 1:15."

If one has to use you-statements, it is best to use them descriptively rather than as interpretations or characterizations of a child's behavior. Table 8.1 shows the difference.

Parents have the responsibility to socialize and direct their children's behaviors. It is difficult and even undesirable to do so without drawing children's attention to their own behavior. Not all you-statements are the same. The most constructive you-statements are those that describe a child's behavior without calling the child's core identity into question.

Task 8.2. Asserting Without Blaming

The biggest obstacle to clear and effective communication in situations involving interpersonal conflict is defensive feelings that arise when someone feels blamed. In interactions between parents and children, it is difficult (but not impossible) to avoid statements that communicate blame. The trick is to discriminate between you-statements and I-statements. You-statements are statements of blame; you-statements point a finger at the other person. I-statements avoid blame by pointing to one's own interests and needs in a situation. You-statements are about what the other person has done wrong; I-statements express how the other's behaviors have affected the self. Whereas you-statements communicate blame, I-statements reveal one's feelings (and even vulnerabilities) to the other person. You can use the diagrams provided here to identify you-statements that you (and your child) tend to use and to brainstorm realistic I-statements that you (and your child) can use instead.

You _____
_____
_____
_____

I _____
_____
_____
_____

You _____

_____

_____

_____

I _____

_____

_____

_____

How Guided Collaboration and Problem Solving Fosters Social Development and Personal Responsibility

Guided collaboration and problem solving can be a powerful tool for fostering social development and personal responsibility. There are many reasons this is the case.

Guided collaboration directly builds perspective-taking skills. When parents guide children through the process of collaborative problem solving, children are required to think about and understand the perspectives of other people. The goal of collaborative problem solving is to work toward win-win solutions. To do this, children must be able to develop a sense of their own interests and the interests of others. Furthermore, they must be able to gain a sense of how their interests are related to the interests of others. When parents guide children through the process of collaborative problem solving, children are forced to move beyond their own interests and address the interests of others head on.

Guided collaboration strengthens the parent–child relationship. So often, when it comes to parent–child interaction, parents and children alike can often think of each other as the enemy. When positions collide, it is hard not to get entrenched in a battle of wills. In any such contest, someone wins and someone loses. However, when a parent guides a child through the process of collaborative problem solving, children gain a deep emotional appreciation that their parents are on their side. They do this as they develop a more complex and nuanced understanding of their relationship to others. They come to appreciate something like: "I understand what my parents want and why they want it. But I also understand that my parents want me to get what I want. They are looking out for me; they are trying to show me the right or effective ways for me to advance my interests." Once a child gets such a sense, they are not only able to develop a deeper respect for their parent's intentions, they may also seek out their parent's advice on matters that other children might keep secret.

Guided collaboration builds personal responsibility. In guided collaboration, children participate in decisions that are made about their actions. When a child agrees to a jointly created solution, he has assumed public responsibility for his part of the agreement. The child knows that the privilege that has been extended to him is conditional on keeping the agreement that has been made. (The parent, of course, is under a similar obligation.) If the child forfeits on the agreement, he must assume responsibility for doing so and accept the consequences that follow his failure to live up to the agreement.

Guided collaboration builds problem-solving skills. When children and parents collaborate to solve a problem, they are in the business of creating solutions. Yes, there may be some obvious solutions to problems that are simply there, waiting to be used. More often than not that is not the case. Frequently, the solutions that are selected are those that neither party has thought of yet, which could not have been created without the participation of both partners. Common ground is not simply found; it is made. As a result, collaborative problem solving is a creative process. Children learn what they do, and especially what they do under the guidance of more accomplished others. When they participate in guided problem solving, they learn how to create novel solutions to complex problems.

Guided collaboration builds social and moral values. The famous communication theorist Marshall McLuhan is known for his phrase, "the medium is the message." This means that not only what we communicate that matters, so does how we communicate it. Guided collaboration is a particular way of communicating. The process presupposes a series of social values that are built into the very process of guided collaboration. These values include respect for the interests of others, reciprocity in social relationships, the need to balance self-assertion with sensitivity to others, taking responsibility for agreements, the value of commitment to a course of action, empathy and compassion for others, the usefulness of thinking outside the box, and more. Again, children learn what they do, especially what they do under the sensitive guidance of others. If this is so, then learning to engage in collaborative problem solving will teach children the social and moral values on which that communicative process is based.

Authoritative Parenting and Moral Character: Timeless Truths in a Changing World

What can I do today to be a better person?

====================

Old-school parenting is authoritative parenting. Authoritative parenting is old-school not because it is old-fashioned, but because it has passed the test of time. It reflects a series of time-honored truths. First, to raise competent, moral and socially successful children, hold children to high moral standards while simultaneously providing the loving and nurturing support they need to attain to those standards. Authoritative parents know that demandingness and responsiveness are not opposite poles of a single dimension. Effective parenting does not require the choice of either being directive or responsive; it requires a commitment to both directiveness and responsiveness.

Second, authoritative parents know that parental authority is legitimate part of their job description. The parent–child relationship is not equal. A parent is not a child's friend or playmate. The parent–child relationship is asymmetrical. Parents have legitimate authority over children by virtue of their greater knowledge and expertise and by virtue of the responsibility that they have to foster their children's development. This is not to say that a parent's authority over a child is total or final. A parent is not a child's boss or master. The boss or master does not act for the well-being of his subordinate. A master acts to advance his own interests, the boss to advance the company's interests. In contrast, a parent uses her authority to advance the child's well-being. It is both her right and her responsibility. Children become equals (or near equals) to their parents when their knowledge and skill comes to meet or exceed those of their parents,[1] or when parents no longer have responsibility to ensure their children's well-being. Over time, sometimes the roles of parents and children reverse, as when children begin to take responsibility for aging parents.

Third, authoritative parents understand that it is through their legitimate authority that they are able to play a role in fostering the development of moral character in their children. Without the authority that comes from their responsibility and expertise—moral or otherwise—parents could not assume a role in directing their children's psychological, social, and moral development.

However, to say that authoritative parenting is timeless does not mean that we can simply look to the past to solve contemporary parenting problems. Even if we embrace that which is old-school about authoritative parenting, as a society we cannot go backward. It is not helpful to romanticize the past. For example, older generations have always found fault with the new. Children have always been lazier, less educated, and less well disciplined than their parents and grandparents. It is hard to resist the conclusion that such old-school complaints are mainly the ruminations of older folks who resist the demise of their ways. If there were old ways that were better than the new ones, it is also true that there were old ways that were worse. We cannot move forward by returning to the past. If we find something valuable in old-school ways, we must nonetheless reinvent those ways to address our current circumstances—even if we are critical of the present.

---

1. Children gain greater expertise in some areas of life long before they become adults. Many 10-year-olds are far more competent in the use of electronic devices than their parents are. Even here, parents have the responsibility to ensure that children are using those devices safely. Expertise in local areas is not sufficient to usurp parental authority. Responsive parents are able to incorporate children's expertise into their parental agendas.

We do not live in a world of moral certainty and stability. We may think that earlier times were simpler and offered greater moral clarity. This is almost certainly the product of a failure in the scope of our vision. There has always been personal, cultural, and moral diversity in the world. Technology has brought us to the point at which we are able to encounter and communicate with others around the globe almost instantaneously. We live in a world in which our beliefs are always subject to change as a result of science, technology, social change, and the clash of cultures and values. Our worlds are "moving and mixing," and as they do, we find ourselves confronting diverse others who cannot help but challenge our sense of social and moral certainty. As a result, it becomes necessary to adapt any timeless truths we claim to have to modern sensibilities.

In what ways is it necessary to update the principles of authoritative parenting and moral self-cultivation in light of our present circumstances? Two points come to mind. Both are based on a timeless truth that is directly relevant to the crisis of moral uncertainty that is a necessary outcome of embracing diversity. First, properly managed, conflict can often be an occasion for development. Where there is diversity, there will often be conflict. Conflict is not necessarily a bad thing; problems arise from how we manage conflict. The principles described in Keys 6–8 show how authoritative parents can foster social development in children by teaching them the art of collaborative problem solving. The values, principles, and procedures of conflict resolution are our best tools for managing social and moral conflicts. Teaching children the art of collaborative problem solving offers the hope that they may be able to create common ground in their interactions with various others, even if their parents had difficulty in this regard.

Second, in the absence of socially shared moral beliefs, it can be difficult for parents to know what social, ethical, and moral beliefs to teach their children. This need not be an intractable problem. All parents have an intuitive sense of what they want for their children, what they feel is right and wrong, and what it means to be a good person. Few parents have it all worked out beforehand. Happily, this is not necessary. The process of moral self-cultivation is not restricted to children; it extends to all of us. If we are uncertain of our moral path, we should feel free to start anywhere. Good tends to beget good. What virtues, values, and principles do we find worthy? Why? We can begin to cultivate those virtues in ourselves and our children. We can test them out in our everyday experience. If they work, we continue to cultivate them. If they fail, we consider revising them. If we run up against people whose values conflict with ours, we can enlist our skills in collaborative problem solving to explore the possibility of creating novel values, or, failing that, at least communicating the desire to be open to the possibility of finding ways to coordinate our interests and values with those of diverse others.

What Do We Ultimately Want for Our Children?

All parents want their children to have a good life. Parents want their children to be happy—in the short and long term. Indeed, Aristotle suggested happiness is the ultimate aim of everything we do. Why do we do the things that we do? Virtually everything we do is "for the sake" of something else. We go to school in order to get a job; we get a job in order to make money; we make money in order to have a home and raise a family. We do all these things for the sake of being happy. Why do we want to be happy? According to Aristotle, happiness is our ultimate aim—the thing we want for its own sake, and not for the sake of anything else.

If we want our children to have a good life, how do we prepare them to do so? If happiness is key to a good life, what will make us happy? This turns out to be a more difficult question than it seems. We often think of happiness as a kind of bodily feeling—a set of pleasurable sensations that occur when we get something that we want. This type of thinking leads to the idea that happiness is about seeking pleasure, a belief expressed in the maxim, "If it feels good, do it." Of course, we know that seeking bodily pleasures is not a formula for a happy life. While a life filled with pleasure may feel good in the moment, the mere fact that something brings pleasure does not mean that it *is* good.[2] Tasty foods consumed in abundance can harm one's health, too much alcohol impedes one's capacity to live a successful life, sexual promiscuity can be harmful to interpersonal relationships, and so on. Once the pleasure of such pursuits fades, people tend to be unfulfilled and left with a sense of emptiness.

We often think that happiness is a kind of goal—something to be sought over time. A few moments of reflection will lead you to see that this simply cannot be the case. People often believe that happiness is something they will achieve when they reach their life goals. "I will be happy when I complete my schooling, find a good job, get married, have a home and a family, retire," and so on. The problem, again, is that the joys of meeting any particular goal are short-lived. After the joy of reaching any particular life goal dissipates, we feel unfulfilled. As a result, we set our minds on the next goal that we believe will bring happiness. Because happiness is always deferred to the next goal, the state of happiness never comes.

What about fame? Does fame bring happiness? Here we have a different problem. A person who seeks fame is at the mercy of the judgments of other people. There are countless examples of people who attain fame but who nonetheless lead difficult and unhappy lives. This is especially true of young celebrities, who must face the question of how to define their self-worth once fame fades. This is not to say that attaining respect from others is not an important goal in life; it is. How-

---

2. The mere fact that a person experiences pleasure from an action does not make that action good. In fact, the philosopher Plato suggested that the first job of parents is to teach children to find pleasure in the right things.

ever, seeking a sense of self-worth through fame makes one's happiness dependent on the shifting approval of others. When this happens, one cedes one's happiness to capricious forces that are beyond one's sphere of control.

If pleasure, personal goals, and fame do not lead to lasting happiness, then what does? To answer this question, we have to realize that the term *happiness* has different meanings. We sometimes use the word to refer to an emotion—to the good feelings that we have when we get something we want. We might say "I am happy" when we are feeling good after a good meal, after receiving a wanted gift, or when we get the job we were seeking. When we think this way, we are led to believe that a good life is one in which we feel happy over long periods. However, a good life is not one that is simply filled with happy feelings. Long-term happiness is not so much a matter of having pleasing or happy sensations over time as it is a matter of being able to make the judgment that our life is good—that is, that we are living a good life. The moment we begin to speak of a good life, we have entered into the world of evaluation and moral judgment. The statement that we are living a good, meaningful, or satisfying life is an evaluative one. It involves using standards of value, worth, or moral goodness to evaluate who we are and what we are doing in our lives. A good life is not good simply because it brings pleasure; it is good because it conforms to our standards of worth, value, or goodness.

What, therefore, leads to a meaningful, happy, and fulfilling life? Again, Aristotle is instructive. To live a happy life, it is necessary to cultivate goodness—moral goodness. For Aristotle, this meant cultivating virtue. To live a good life, it is necessary to work toward becoming a good person and contribute to the good in the world. This means that we cannot lead a good life in the absence of some sort of moral framework that can help us define what it means to be good. If we want our children to live good and happy lives, we must help them identify themselves in terms of values that define what it means to become a good person. This means helping children cultivate moral character.

The Fall and Rise of Moral Character

The United States was founded on principles of freedom, individual rights, and autonomy. From the early days of the republic (indeed, in the Declaration of Independence), we have recognized individual persons as having rights to "life, liberty and the pursuit of happiness." As a moral system, the U.S. system of individual rights tells us that we are free to pursue our own agendas as long as we do not intrude on the freedoms and rights of others. As a moral system, the notion of individual rights guards us against arbitrary intrusion of others, especially the state. The doctrine of individual rights tells us what other people (and the state) cannot do to us—they cannot infringe on our capacity to speak freely, assemble, vote, and so on. However, with the exception of the call to respect others, the doctrine of individual rights is all but silent in specifying how we *should* relate to other people. While we are obligated not to hurt others, we have no special obligations or duties to care for each other. Our relations to each other are largely matters of free choice or social contract.

It is easy to imagine that accepting the principles of freedom, autonomy, and individual rights might produce a society in which people seek to fulfill their own personal happiness without regard for the interests and needs of others. However, from the early days of the republic, unmitigated freedom was held in check by a series of voluntary constraints. From its inception, the concept of individual freedom had strong ties to the notion of responsibility. Freedom carried with it a presumption that one should be responsible to others; there could be no rights without responsibilities. Furthermore, unrestricted freedom was held in check by shared community standards, strong expectations of personal and civic virtue, and the waxing and waning influences of religion. Moral character was supported by the existence of more or less shared systems of values for regulating personal and moral conduct.

Since the founding of the United States, however, there has been a steady decline in the value that parents place on obedience to moral norms and a corresponding increase in the value that parents place on personal autonomy. In the early days, these were particularly welcome changes, as the value of obedience was often expressed in authoritarian parenting practices. Beginning in the early 1900s, the child-centered movement promulgated values of autonomy, creativity, and individual initiative over conformity to rigid rule systems. The movement toward increasing individualism was hastened in the years after the 1950s, when American culture experienced a tumultuous period of questioning received authority and traditional values. The 1960s inaugurated a long period that has resulted in a suite of positive social changes directed toward empowering individuals. These include but are not limited to civil, women's, and lesbian/gay/bisexual/transgender rights; increased concern with diversity; and greater tolerance of different moral perspectives and belief systems.

It is rarely helpful to characterize any given epoch in history as either all good or all bad; there are necessarily positive and negative qualities associated with any series of historical changes. During the last half of the twentieth century, the same forces that led to the questioning of traditional values, the loss of faith in dominant institutions, and increased toleration of diversity also produced a state of social and moral uncertainty. As faith in traditional moral views waned, so did the concept of moral character. For better or worse, in periods, Americans were more likely to define themselves with reference to standards of virtue and moral goodness. The question of "who I ought to be" was more central to a person's sense of self. Children and adults alike were more likely to define themselves in terms of public virtues such as hard work, compassion, thrift, self-discipline, honesty, perseverance, and so forth. In so doing, they were more likely to hold themselves accountable to public standards. Attaining or violating shared moral standards had implications for an individual's sense of self and could bring about social emotions such as pride, honor, guilt, or shame.

Recent advances in technology and electronic communications have reinforced and even exacerbated such uncertainty. We have the ability to obtain instant information about virtually anything at virtually any time. As we increasingly encounter different people, different cultures, and different values from around the world, we appropriately begin to question our own. Against the backdrop of a diverse and changing world, it is difficult to hold onto certainties about who we are and who we should be.

The result has been an increasing severing of personal selfhood from public virtue (see Figure 9.1). As Americans have lost faith in public institutions, they have become less likely to identify themselves in terms of moral character and public virtue and more likely to define themselves in terms of per-

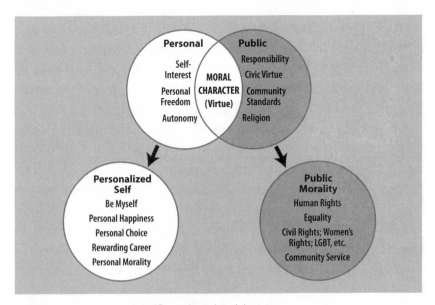

Figure 9.1. Personal Selfhood and Public Virtue

sonal goals, pragmatic pursuits, and self-selected identifica-
tions. Within our interpersonal interactions, public virtue has
given way to a kind of personalized morality; in the absence of
single moral system that is equally binding for everyone, we
seem to believe that the best we can do is to honor the right of
each individual to make moral decisions himself. Such a situation has led to a state of affairs embracing either radical tolerance of alternative moral systems (i.e., moral relativism) or
massive polarization between encased moral positions. We
seem to fluctuate between "Who am I to impose my moral
system onto you?" and "My moral system is right and yours is
wrong." At the same time, moral life is has been increasingly
relegated to the public sphere, where it is concerned primarily
with programs for promoting the equality, choice, and well-
being of individuals.

Reinventing Moral Character

As it becomes increasingly clear that the pendulum has swung
too far in the direction of individual autonomy rather than
moral concern for others, policy makers, educators, and profes-
sionals have increasingly called for the restoration of moral
character in children. What will it take to restore character
development as a goal of child rearing? What will it take to
redirect children's social development in the direction of moral
character rather than toward increasing self-focus?

Many of the ideas and recommendations put forth in this
book follow from another timeless truth: Socially competent
children (and adults) are those who are able to assert their own
interests while simultaneously taking into consideration the
interests of others. Any social interaction is made up of at least
two people. Each of those individuals has interests. The key to
successful social relations is the capacity to coordinate one's
own interests with those of another person. This idea has direct
implications for promoting moral character in children. All of
us—children and adults included—experience two different

types of motives: self-interest and concern for others. People act out of self-interest when they pursue food due to hunger and thirst, pursue their own personal goals, seek fame and fortune, and so on. We act out of concern for others when we help other people, share our food, compliment a friend's accomplishment, or otherwise act for the benefit of other people. Concern for others is the basis of all forms of moral conduct. If it were not for the presence of other people, moral concerns would not ordinarily arise.

The key to fostering the development of moral character is helping children build a bridge between their self-interests and their concerns for the interests of others. Children and adults who act in morally exemplary ways are those who have formed a moral identity—a sense of self in which concern for the welfare of others plays a central role. Such individuals gain a sense of satisfaction by acting out their commitment to some sort of moral code—particularly those that involve concern for others. They measure themselves in terms of what they can do for others, how they can contribute to the world, how they can become better and make the world better—not simply in terms of what others can do for them. This is not to say that forging a moral identity involves denying self-interest. On the contrary—acting on the basis of a moral identity is not a matter of repressing one's interests; it enhances and transforms them. To have a moral identity is to internalize standards for what it means to be a good person, and thus to make those standards my own. It thus becomes my interest to act on the basis of those standards. It becomes my interest not in the sense that "I will gain more for myself" if I act morally, but because living out my moral identity helps me become who I am and who I want to be.

When children are very young, their experience of self-interest and feelings of concern for others tend to be separate. In some situations, children act out of self-interest; in others, they may act out of concern for others. For example, if Tim wants Lexi's toy, he may simply grab it. If, on another occasion, Tim sees Lexi cry over when her toy breaks, he might attempt

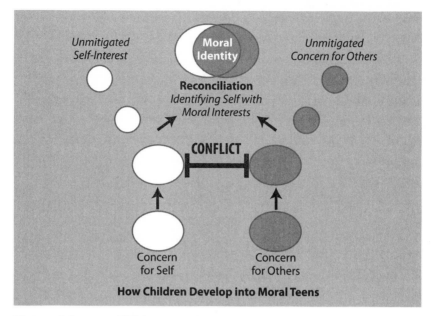

Figure 9.2. How Children Develop into Moral Teens

to comfort Lexi, fix her toy, or give her another one. Children tend to switch from self-interest to concern for others from moment to moment. This phase of development is shown by the separate circles representing self-interest and concern for others at the bottom of Figure 9.2.

For young children, if there is a conflict between self-interest (Tim wants the toy) and care for others (Lexi wants the same toy), they will often—but not always—take the path of self-interest. Soon, however—especially when adults call it to their attention—children will become explicitly aware of the conflict between their self-interest and concern for others. They can begin to see, "If I take the toy, I'll get what I want; but if I take the toy, my friend will be sad. What should I do?" This is shown in the middle of Figure 9.2.

What's important here is how children deal with this conflict over time. Once they are able to hold in mind the contradiction between their own desires and the desires of others, they can begin to face the task of what to do about it. Over time, children can manage this contradiction in many ways. As shown in Figure 9.2, children can develop in at least three different directions depending on how they resolve this question. Allowing self-interest to dominate over concern for others, children can develop in the direction of unmitigated self-interest; choosing to defer self-interest to others, they can develop in the direction of unmitigated concern for others. The third option is to reconcile self-interest with concern for others. In such reconciliation, children bring their self-interest and their concern for others together to form a moral identity.

When forging a moral identity, children come to identify themselves with the goal of acting out of concern for others. By the time they enter adolescence, instead of seeing concern for others as something that is at odds with self-interest, they can come to see that acting out of care for others can be part of who they are. They will have forged a moral identity and will become more likely to act from a sense of purpose rather than simply from a sense of self-interest. Helping children reconcile self-interest with concern for others is a key process in fostering self-cultivation and the formation of moral character.

How Parents Help Children Complete Themselves

Parents can play a central role in helping children cultivate moral character. If we are to reverse the unwanted effects of indulgent, permissive, and child-centered approaches to parenting, we must rethink our everyday notions about how character develops and how parents foster character development.

As discussed in earlier chapters, the task of fostering character in children means putting them on the path to moral self-cultivation. Moral self-cultivation is the life-long process of incremental self-improvement and self-appreciation over time. It involves (1) continuously reflecting on who one believes one

Figure 9.3. Who Am I?

should be, (2) acting to revise one's behavior in ways that conform to one's images of worth, while simultaneously (3) appreciating the value of oneself in the present. Moral self-cultivation is a process that involves self-reflection. It is a process in which children reflect on themselves and who they wish to become. It involves reflecting on oneself and building a kind of theory of "who I am" and "who I want to become" (see Figure 9.3)

In teaching the art of moral self-cultivation, the first job of the parent is to help prompt children to engage in the process of moral reflection. The goal is to teach children to ask themselves questions like, "Who do I want to be?" "Who should I become?" "What does it mean to be a good person?" "What is the right thing to do in this situation?" "Are they doing the right thing?" "Why?" The best way to do this is to ask children these questions in everyday concrete situations and guide them through the process of answering. Over time, the goal is to encourage children to ask themselves something like, "What can I do today to make myself a better person?" rather than simply, "What can I do today that will make me happy?"

To foster the cultivation of character in children, parents must believe that character is something over which they can and should have an influence. This will require that we rethink the child-centered approach to parenting. Child-centered parents tend to adopt the belief that that character and moral beliefs are things that must come primarily from the child himself. This view tends to takes two different forms. The first view is that character is something that has its origins deep within a child (see Figure 9.4).

From this point of view, a child's sense of self is found by looking inward. This view has a long history in American culture. It is consistent with the ideas of individual autonomy and self-determination. To be autonomous and independent is to be true to oneself, which is seen as a process of looking within to find out who one truly is and what one truly believes. A few moments of reflection reveals that this cannot be the case. Moral character is not something that can be found by simply looking within one's self. When I search my own experience, I may be aware that I feel hungry, irritable, calm, excited, or anxious—but I cannot search within myself and conclude that I am thrifty, courageous, kind, hard-working, or caring. These are not fixed qualities that exist inside of me; they are the results of what I do over time. They are social and moral values that I must identify with and cultivate over time. Moral character is not a synonym for personality; moral character is something

Figure 9.4. Who I Am Comes from Within

Figure 9.5. Choose for Yourself

that is acquired over time through interactions with others. It is not an inner thing that can be searched and discovered by oneself.

The second view, again consistent with a child-centered approach, acknowledges that "who I am" is not something that is found by looking within. Instead, it acknowledges character and moral beliefs are something that are acquired over time. Some parents believe, however, that character and moral beliefs are something that must ultimately be chosen by the child herself (see Figure 9.5)

However, like child-centered parenting itself, this way of thinking is only partially correct. Although it is true that children ultimately must decide what they believe and who they wish to become for themselves, it is not true that they create who they are *by* themselves. Children need guidance from responsible and accomplished adults about how to craft a worthy self. No one would suggest that children be left on their own to decide how to fly a plane or perform a medical operation. It makes little sense to leave children to their own devices when they embark on the even more difficult task of forging a moral self. As they grow, many different value systems will make themselves available. Do I study hard or skip homework to play with friends? Do I make fun of the different kid or offer a compassionate hand? Do I brag about my accomplishments or do I remain humble? Children will witness peers who embrace the values of each of these ways of being in the world. They need guidance to understand the implications of embracing any particular way of being. If the guidance does not come from parents, it will come from other sources.

The alternatives to child-centered parenting include adult-centered approaches that place strict limits on a child's capacity to influence the course of his own development. From a strictly adult-centered point of view, a child's sense of identity comes from outside rather than from within the child (see Figure 9.6).

This strategy is adopted by authoritarian parents who seek to influence children without providing support for their developing needs for autonomy. Although parental involvement is crucial in fostering the development character and moral identity in children, children are not lumps of clay who can be molded according to a parent's whim. A child's existing dispositions and preferences not only influence the course of her development, they also influence how parents treat children. To be influenced by parents, children must internalize parental standards.

Figure 9.6. Who I Am Comes from Outside

This does not happen unless parents are responsive to their children's emotional needs and dispositions and make room for them to modify parental standards as they internalize them and make them their own.

Moral character neither springs forward from within a child nor is something that can be simply imposed from the outside. Instead, moral character is something that develops through the thousands of interactions that occur between children and other people, most particularly parents, adults, and influential peers (see Figure 9.7)

Children bring their existing goals, emotions, strengths, vulnerabilities, preferences, and dispositions to any interaction of which they are a part. As a result, although parents influence their children, children also influence their parents. Authoritative parents are responsive to children's dispositions as they guide children in the direction of moral growth. For example, Sam may find that he likes to play soccer, but that he does not like math. Soccer comes easily, but math is difficult. Sam's mother, wanting to support the development of her son's interests, builds on them. In an attempt to foster character development, she uses Sam's interests to promote the value of perseverance, collaboration, or humility. For example, she may draw on the example of Sam's existing tendency to persevere and improve

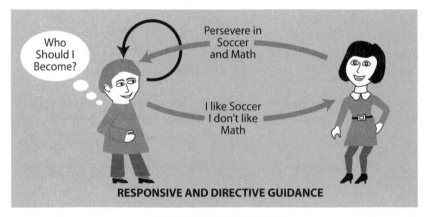

Figure 9.7. Responsive and Directive Guidance

in soccer when coaching him to persevere during his math homework. Alternatively, she may draw analogies between the need for teamwork in soccer to stress the need to seek help and work collaboratively with teachers or tutors to support the development of math skills. She may stress the importance of humility before others when Sam does well in soccer by calling attention to the difficulties that he has in building skills in mathematics.

What Can I Do Today to Become a Better Person?

It may seem like something of a paradox, but it is nonetheless true. If we want our children to lead happy and meaningful lives, instead of encouraging children to ask, "What can I do today to make myself happy?," it might be better to teach them to ask, "What can I do today to make myself a better person?" This is the essence of moral self-cultivation. As we encourage our children to grow, it is equally important to teach them the art of self-appreciation. This involves teaching them to ask themselves, "What can I find of value in who I have become today?" Even very young children can understand these old-school values. Cultivating a self is much like cultivating a garden. It involves both effortful action and reflective appreciation. Consider how these ideas are expressed in the classic children's folk song, "Oats Peas Beans and Barley Grow":

> Oats, peas, beans, and barley grow.
> Oats, peas, beans, and barley grow.
> Can you or I or anyone know
> How oats, peas, beans, and barley grow?
>
> First the farmer sows his seed,
> Stands erect and takes his ease,
> He stamps his foot and claps his hands,
> And turns around to view his lands.

Next the farmer waters the seed,
Stands erect and takes his ease,
He stamps his foot and claps his hands,
And turns around to view his lands.

Next the farmer hoes the weeds,
Stands erect and takes his ease,
He stamps his foot and claps his hands,
And turns around to view his lands.

Last the farmer harvests his seed,
Stands erect and takes his ease,
He stamps his foot and claps his hands,
And turns around to view his lands.

Appendix: A Real-Life Example of Guiding Children through Conflict Management

The interchange provided in this appendix illustrates many of the strategies for guiding children through the process of conflict management that are discussed in this book. These include managing emotions, helping children articulate their interests and needs without blame, negotiating from interests, using I-statements and avoiding you-statements, active listening, fostering empathy, and creating win-win solutions. In this situation, with the assistance of a mediator, a mother guides her daughters through the process of resolving a conflict that occurred between them the previous day. The girls were playing an Internet computer game (Animal Jam) in which players seek to obtain a series of virtual animals. In this situation, 10-year-old Alison earned an Arctic Wolf and an Eagle as part of her game play. Her sister, seven-year-old Evelyn, became upset (jealous) because she had not yet earned these virtual animals.

In reflecting on the evens of the previous night, assisted by the adults, the girls worked through their conflict. Evelyn was able to explain to her older sister that she felt "angry" that Alison had earned an Arctic Wolf and an Eagle when Evelyn had not. Under the guidance of the mediator and the girls' mother, Alison was able to understand and empathize with Evelyn's jealous feelings, and Evelyn was able to understand that Alison had done nothing wrong to Evelyn simply by earning the virtual game animals.

Appendix Table 1

Conversation	Explanation
Mom: Can you tell Alison what made you upset last night?	Mom asks Evelyn to describe what happened.
Evelyn: [*Very soft and sad*] You got an Arctic Wolf and an Eagle.	Although Alison could experience "You got" as blame, Evelyn describes what happened with minimal blaming language.
Alison: I know! . . .	
Mom: Explain to her why. Why were you so upset?	Mom encourages Evelyn to explain why she felt upset.
Alison: Why were you so upset over animals?	Alison is mildly defensive and implies that Evelyn perhaps shouldn't have been so upset.
Evelyn: Because I never ever ever ever got an Eagle or an Arctic Wolf.	Evelyn provides her reason using an I-statement.
Alison: [*Pause*] There's a first time for everything.	Alison takes some time to figure out how to respond. She seems to be balancing how to be compassionate to Evelyn while also not taking responsibility for what happened to Evelyn.

Describing What Happened
(Using Descriptive not Evaluative Terms)

In this first set of exchanges (see Appendix Table 1), the girls' mother guides Evelyn through the process of describing what happened the previous evening while stating her interests and feelings to her sister.

Disclosing Feelings (I-Statements not You-Statements)

In the previous exchange, Evelyn described what happened, but did not describe her feelings, even though her mother had explicitly asked her how she felt. The mediator then attempted to guide Evelyn through the process of expressing how she felt when her sister received a prize and she didn't (Appendix Table 2).

Appendix Table 2

Conversation	Explanation
Mediator: How did you feel, Evelyn, when she got the [Arctic Wolf]?	Mediator asks Eveyln to disclose her feelings.
Evelyn: I was really really angry and sad.	Evelyn uses I-statements to disclose her emotions
Mediator: You were angry and sad. Do you know what it means to be jealous? [Evelyn: No] You don't know what it means to be jealous, to want something that someone else has? Evelyn: No.	Sensing that Evelyn might have been jealous rather than simply angry, the mediator asks if she knows what jealousy is. When Evelyn shows that she doesn't know, the mediator moves on.
Mediator: You were angry and sad at her . . . yeah . . . What would you like to have happen?	Mediator is attempting to help Evelyn identify her interests in the situation.
Evelyn: I would have liked it if we both got an Arctic Wolf.	The mediator was not clear enough in his question. Evelyn thought the question was about the prize she wanted. The mediator should have asked what Evelyn wanted from Alison.
Mediator: Uh huh . . . Who were you angry at?	Mediator tries to get Evelyn to focus on her feelings about Alison.

Summarizing Interests and Feelings

After Evelyn describes her feelings, her mother restates what Evelyn said back to her. Immediately, Evelyn shows emotional signs of relief in feeling understood (Appendix Table 3).

Helping Children Appreciate Each Other's Interests and Feelings

In an attempt to help Evelyn elaborate her feelings more clearly, the mediator asks her to explain her interests in this situation—that is, what she wanted from Alison that would make the situation better (Appendix Table 4). Evelyn says that she wanted Alison to say "sorry." At this point, the conflict between the sisters becomes apparent. Evelyn wants Alison to

Appendix Table 3

Conversation	Explanation
Mom: Evelyn what did you spend your diamonds on, when you got your membership?	Mom tries to find out why Evelyn didn't have enough diamonds of her own to purchase an Eagle or Arctic Wolf in the game.
Evelyn: They didn't put diamonds on the membership card.	
Mom: Oh, so that's why you're jealous, because you didn't get diamonds on your membership.	Mom summarizes and extends Evelyn's explanation for why she couldn't get the prize she wanted.
Evelyn: Mm hm.	Evelyn feels understood and expresses it with enthusiasm.
Mom: And they changed it since then.	
Evelyn: Mm hm.	Evelyn feels understood and expresses it with feeling.

apologize for getting a prize when Evelyn did not. She wants Alison to delete her Arctic Wolf to make things fair. Although Evelyn says that she feels "angry" and "sad," the mediator sensed that Evelyn may have been feeling jealous but did not yet understand the concept of jealousy. The mediator now has the job of helping Evelyn express her feelings without making Alison feel blamed for doing something wrong. The mediator does this by giving Alison a turn to express how she felt about Evelyn's desire that she apologize. Once both children are able to calmly describe their feelings to each other, they are in a position to understand each other's interests—even if they don't agree with each other. This is not something that children are able to do well on their own. If, however, each child feels that she is has been able to express her feelings and be understood (at least by the parent), the chances of creating a solution to the conflict are greatly enhanced.

In this situation, Evelyn and Alison are able to express their interests and feelings and be understood by the mediator. As a result, they are able to keep their emotions in check. The mediator is thus able to help Evelyn and Alison begin to understand each other's feelings and interests.

Appendix Table 4

Conversation	Explanation
Mediator: When you were upset, Evelyn, what did you want from Alison? Did you want Alison to do something?	Mediator again tries to help Evelyn identify her interests (what she wants) in the situation.
Evelyn: I wanted her to say sorry and I . . .	Evelyn is able to express what she wanted from Alison.
Alison: [Defensive] She wanted me to delete the Arctic Wolf.	Alison, presumably feeling a bit blamed by Evelyn's request, becomes slightly defensive.
Evelyn: Because then it would be fair. [soft and sad]	Evelyn completes her thought.
Mediator: [To Alison] Why do you think she wanted you to delete your Arctic Wolf?	Mediator attempts to help Alison understand Evelyn's feelings and interests—even if Alison may not agree with them.
Alison: Because she didn't want me to have it when she didn't have it . . . but when she got it I could have made her delete hers. . . see? It just wouldn't work out.	Alison shows a clear understanding of Evelyn's jealousy. She also shows an understanding of reciprocity—if Alison has to delete her Arctic Wolf, then if Evelyn were to get one herself, Alison could ask Evelyn to delete hers, too—a lose-lose situation.
Mediator: Hmm, right, right . . . How did you feel when she wanted you to delete your Arctic Wolf?	Mediator attempts to help Alison identify her feelings—especially feelings of being blamed by Evelyn.
Alison: Really hurt	Alison is able to express her feelings clearly.
Mediator: So, you were angry, Evelyn, and sad that you didn't get the Arctic Wolf. And Alison, you were kind of angry that she would want you to . . .	Mediator brings both Eveyln's and Alison's interests together at the same time so that both could hear each other's interest and feel understood at the same time.
Alison: Delete it, yeah [feeling understood]	
Mediator: Delete it . . . but did you hear. . . did you hear what [softer, compassionately] Evelyn wanted? Do you remember what she wanted? Tell her again what you wanted, Evelyn.	Mediator focuses on helping Alison understand Evelyn's interest (to be consoled about feeling jealous about Alison's prize). The mediator asks Evelyn to articulate her interests directly to Alison.

(continued)

Appendix Table 4 Continued

Conversation	Explanation
Evelyn: I wanted an Arctic Wolf and an Eagle, but I couldn't have gotten that for her.	Again, the mediator was unclear about what he was asking Evelyn. He wanted her to express her desire to be consoled (and not to get the prizes).
Mediator: I remember her saying that you wanted to feel, that you wanted, Evelyn, Alison to say she is sorry. Is that what you said?	The mediator articulate Evelyn's previously stated interest to have Alison say she was sorry.
Alison: Sorry.	Alison immediately interjects "sorry," even though she did nothing wrong.
Mediator: Is that what you said?	Mediator ensures that he understood Evelyn's previously stated interest correctly.
Evelyn: Mm hm.	Evelyn clearly feels understood.

Separating Person (Blaming) from Problem (Underlying Interests)

Evelyn feels understood in this situation, but Alison does not. Even though she apologized to Evelyn, it seems as though she may have done so out of a sense of compassion, obligation, or both. As a result, she hides under a set of large couch pillows. The mediator now attempts to acknowledge Alison's feelings of being blamed. He also tries to show Evelyn that even though she said "sorry," Alison didn't do anything wrong.

Alison, feeling understood, comes out from under the pillows.

Coordinating Underlying Interests

At this point, both Evelyn and Alison have been able to express their interests and feelings and be understood by the mediator. As a result, they are able to keep their emotions in check. The mediator is thus able to help the sisters begin to understand each other's feelings and interests (Appendix Table 6).

Appendix Table 5

Conversation	Explanation
Mediator: [*to Alison*] What would it have been like to say sorry for that . . . Alison, hiding person . . . [*Alison is hiding under the pillows with her hands over her ears, blocking out the sound*] Would you have wanted to say "sorry"? . . . Big girl? I wouldn't have wanted to say sorry. I wouldn't have wanted to say sorry because I didn't do anything wrong. . . . If I were you, I woudn't have wanted to say sorry, because I didn't do anything wrong!	Alison is hiding under the pillows. Given her unnecessary apology, the mediator guesses that she is feeling blamed (and perhaps ashamed). The mediator shows empathy for Alison's feelings, stating that he wouldn't want to have said "sorry" for for having done nothing wrong.
Alison: I guess you're right. [*understood*]	When Alison hears the mediator's empathic statement, she stops hiding and agrees with the mediator.
Mediator: Yeah. I wouldn't have wanted to say sorry. . . . But Evelyn was feeling upset about something that you didn't even do.	Mediator continues to reinforce his empathic statement.

Creating a Win-Win Solution to the Problem (Conflict)

Throughout the next exchange (Appendix Table 7), Alison is able to understand and empathize more deeply with Evelyn's feelings of jealousy, while also being clearly aware that she (Alison) is not being blamed. Similarly, Evelyn is able to ask Alison for consolation even though she is aware that Alison did nothing wrong to provoke Evelyn's jealous (i.e., "angry" and "sad" feelings).

Throughout these exchanges, the problem (conflict) between the girls is largely one of hurt feelings brought about by misunderstandings. Over the course of the guided interaction, a win-win solution emerged to their conflict in which each child was able to get what she wanted (interest) from the other (Evelyn wanted to be consoled; Alison wanted to be absolved of blame). This was possible because although the girls' initial positions were in conflict (Evelyn wanted Alison to delete her virtual

Appendix Table 6

Conversation	Explanation
Alison: [*To Evelyn*] Then you should say sorry.	Alison takes the opportunity to blame Evelyn for the situation.
Mediator: Who do you think should say sorry?	The mediator attempts to prompt the children to figure out if saying sorry is helpful in the situation.
Evelyn: Both of us!	Evelyn's response divides the blame equally.
Mediator: Both of you?	The mediator calls for further reflection.
Evelyn: Yeah!	
Mediator: That's an interesting answer. I would say, "both of you or . . . none of you!"	The mediator builds on Evelyn's response (both should say sorry) but also states the opposite (none of you) as an option.
Evelyn: Mmmm? [*Wrinkling her eyebrows in confusion*]	Evelyn is confused by the obvious contradiction in what the mediator has said. Curious, she attends carefully to what the mediator is about to say.
Mediator: None of you, perhaps! But what could . . . You were feeling sad . . . what do you say when you feel sad? What do you want when you feel sad? If I felt sad, what would you do for me?	The mediator attempts to show Evelyn and Alison that even though Alison didn't do anything wrong, if Evelyn was sad, it would still be okay for Evelyn to want to be consoled. The mediator does this by first trying to get Evelyn to identify an appropriate response to someone else's sadness.
Evelyn: Sad [*feeling as if she is being blamed.*	Not yet understanding what the mediator was trying to explain, feeling slightly defensive, Evelyn answers.
Mediator: If Alison were sad, what would you do for her?	The mediator continues to help Evelyn identify an appropriate way to console someone who is sad. He is suggesting that it is appropriate to want to be consoled when one is sad, even if the other person has done nothing wrong.
Evelyn: [*Pauses*]	Evelyn is having difficulty thinking of an answer.
Mediator: Let's say that Alison had a glitch in her computer and it deleted her Wolf. She was crying. What would you want to do for her?	The mediator uses a concrete example to induce a sense of empathy in Evelyn. He is attempting to help her articulate her own desire to receive sympathy rather than an apology from Alison.
Evelyn: [*Sad*] I would want to give her a gift card.	Evelyn proposes an empathetic solution.

Appendix Table 7

Conversation	Explanation
Mom: What do you think Alison	Mother prompts Alison to consider how she might respond to Evelyn.
Mediator: It sounds to me . . .Tell me if I'm right, Evelyn, would it have made you feel good if Alison just gave you a hug, or said, "That's too bad, I wish you got a wolf." Would that have made you feel better?	While directing his statement to Evelyn, the mediator models a possible way that Alison could choose to respond.
Evelyn: Mm hm [*rising intonation at end*].	Evelyn affirms the mediator's suggested using her baby voice.
Mediator: Wow . . . I don't know if Alison would do that or not. But you could ask her. And she may . . .	Addressing Evelyn, the mediator suggests that Alison has a choice of what she might say to Evelyn.
Alison: It's too bad that you didn't get a Wolf, Evelyn.	Alison chooses to comfort Evelyn using words similar to the mediator's.
Mediator: Oh my!	The mediator communicates his positive evaluation of Alison's behavior.
Alison: But you just have to work up to it! Maybe we could find a way to fix that glitch if you still have it [*inaudible*].	Alison gives Evelyn advice about what she has to do to receive one of the game prizes.
Mediator: You know what's important to me? I'm impressed that Alison wanted to help to make you feel good after you felt sad. I think it's important, Alison . . . I think you felt that you were being blamed before for getting the Wolf.	The mediator is concerned that Alison may still be feeling blamed by having been asked to say (and actually having had said) sorry. Worrying that feelings of blame may cause resentment, the mediator seeks to ensure that Alison understands that she was not to blame for Evelyn's distress.
Alison: Mm hmm. And the Eagle.	By adding the Eagle to the mediator's list, Alison suggests that she did in fact feel some blame.
Mediator: Alison, can you tell Evelyn that?	The mediator attempts to show both girls that it is possible for Alison to be sympathetic toward Evelyn, even if she didn't do anything wrong.

(*continued*)

Appendix Table 7 Continued

Conversation	Explanation
Alison: I felt that you were blaming me, Evelyn, though I didn't do anything when I got the Eagle and the Arctic Wolf 'cause I got them and that's it! It's not like . . .	Alison is able to express her feelings using I-statements (without blame).
Mediator: How did you feel about Evelyn being sad?	The mediator wants to ensure that Evelyn understands that even though Alison doesn't want to be blamed, she still feels sympathetic toward Evelyn.
Alison: I was a bit shocked! I didn't know they were the animals she wanted.	The mediator had expected Alison to state that she felt sad for Evelyn; however, Alison explains that she didn't anticipate that Evelyn would be upset.
Evelyn: Those were, Alison [*resolute, slightly blaming*].	Evelyn states emphatically and a defensively that she did indeed want the Arctic Wolf and the Eagle prizes.
Mediator: So . . . Alison felt sad about Evelyn being sad. Look at that big smile [Evelyn], are you happy that she felt sad—are you happy that she cared about you? [Evelyn smiles and laughs, "yeah!"] Evelyn, do you understand what Alison said that she didn't do anything wrong?	The mediator attempts to show Evelyn that Alison felt sad for her. When Evelyn hears this, she becomes visibly pleased. The mediator then attempts to reinforce the idea that it was possible for Alison to feel sad for Evelyn even though Alison did nothing wrong.
Evelyn: Uh huh!	Eveyln responds with understanding.

animals to make things "fair"; since she didn't do anything wrong, Alison wanted to keep her virtual animals), their underlying interests did not conflict. Evelyn's desire to be consoled did not conflict with Alison's legitimate interest in being absolved of blame.

Teaching Children to Understand Emotions

As the interaction waned, the girls' mother sought to resolve the issue of fairness and blame in the interaction. As they dis-

Appendix Table 8

Conversation	Explanation
Mom: Do you think it is fair to get mad at Alison because she got something cool?	Mother tries to further make this point.
Evelyn: Kind of?	Evelyn says that it would be okay to be mad if someone "got something cool" and she did not.
Mom: Really? What if you got something really cool for your birthday that Alison didn't have. Would it be okay for Alison to get mad at you because you got it for your birthday?	Mother is surprised and doesn't understand why Evelyn would say that it was appropriate to become angry at someone if they did nothing wrong. The mother presses further by reversing the roles— asking if it would be okay for Alison to become angry if Evelyn "got something cool" and Alison did not.
Evelyn: Kind of.	Evelyn answer is consistent with her previous response.
Mom: What would you say to Alison if that happened?	Still attempting to understand Evelyn's view, the mother asks how Evelyn would respond to Alison's anger.
Evelyn: Sorry.	Evelyn's answer remains consistent with her belief that anger is justified someone "gets something cool."
Mom: Sorry for what? [*sad tone*] [Evelyn: "Sorry for . . ."] 'Cause you didn't do anything, did you, you got a present. That's what happened with Alison, she used a birthday present money to get her membership.	Mother probes further, and explains why she thinks anger is not appropriate when "someone gets something cool."
Mediator: I'm wondering if angry and jealous are like this, and that it's okay to be jealous and then when you are jealous you get angry. You know what I'm saying?	The mediator suggests that Evelyn is using the word *anger* where the term *jealous* might be more appropriate—that is, that Evelyn is unable to discriminate anger from jealousy.
Mom: Does that make sense?	Mother asks Evelyn if the mediator is correct.
Evelyn: Yeah. [*rising*]	

(continued)

Appendix Table 8 Continued

Conversation	Explanation
Mom: How do you feel now?	Mother probes how Evelyin is feeling.
Evelyn: Mmmm . . . okay. [*rising*]	Evelyn feels better.
Mom: Are you still angry?	After having heard the mediator's distinction between anger and jealousy, Mother asks if Evelyn still feels angry.
Evelyn: A little bit sad still.	Evelyn reports feeling sad rather than angry, perhaps beginning to appreciate the difference between anger and jealousy.
Mediator: Sure, I be sad if I didn't get the Eagle and the Wolf I wanted. How does it feel to know that Alison is sad that you didn't get your Wolf?	The mediator responds empathetically to Evelyn, and then accentuates the idea that Alison felt sad for Evelyn.
Mom: Does it make you feel better that she's sad for you? Or does it make you feel worse?	The mother does the same.
Evelyn: It makes me feel a little better	
Mom: Oh. Why is that?	Mother attempts to see if Evelyn understands why her feelings have changed.
Evelyn: I don't know.	
Mom: Is it maybe because that's how you know she cares about you?	Mother suggests links Evelyn's feeling better to Alison's sympathy for her situation.

cussed Evelyn's feelings, it became clear that Evelyn continued to feel that her anger at Alison was legitimate (Appendix Table 8). This provided an occasion to reflect on the meaning of emotion words and begin to teach Evelyn about the meaning of jealousy and empathy.

At the end of their exchange, Evelyn has been able to both acknowledge and feel good about Alison's feelings of empathy for her. From interactions like these, children develop the capacity to reflect on, make sense of, and act on emotional feelings.

References

Authoritative Parenting

Baumrind, D. (2012). Differentiating between confrontive and coercive kinds of parental power-assertive disciplinary practices. *Human Development*, 55(2), 35–51.

Baumrind, D. (1971). Current patterns of parental authority. *Developmental Psychology*, 4(1, Pt. 2), 1–103.

Larelere, R. E., Morris, A. S., & Hurst, A. W. (Eds.) (2012). *Authoritative Parenting: Synthesizing Nurturance and Discipline for Optimnal Child Development*. Washington, DC: APA Press.

Supporting Children's Autonomy Development

Lekes, N., Gingras, I., Philippe, F. L., Koestner, R., & Fang, J. (2010). Parental autonomy-support, intrinsic life goals, and well-being among adolescents in China and North America. *Journal of Youth & Adolescence*, 39(8), 858–869.

Thomassin, K., & Suveg, C. (2012). Parental autonomy support moderates the link between ADHD symptomatology and task perseverance. *Child Psychiatry and Human Development*, 43(6), 958–967. doi:10.1007/s10578-012-0306-1.

Problems with Child-Centered Parenting and Teaching

Damon, W. (1995). *Greater Expectations: Overcoming the Culture of Indulgence in America's Homes and Schools*. New York: Free Press.

Mascolo, M. F. (2009). Beyond teacher- and learner-centered pedagogy: Learning as guided participation. *Pedagogy and the Human Sciences, 1,* 4–27.

Ochs, E., & Izquierdo, C. (2009). Responsibility in childhood: Three developmental trajectories. *Ethos,* 37(4), 391–413.

Narcissism and Self-Focus in Contemporary Children

Twenge, J. M., Konrath, S., Foster, J. D., Keith Campbell, W. W., & Bushman, B. J. (2008). Egos inflating over time: A cross-temporal meta-analysis of the Narcissistic Personality Inventory. *Journal of Personality,* 76(4), 875–902.

Twenge, J. M., Konrath, S., Foster, J. D., Campbell, W., & Bushman, B. J. (2008). Further evidence of an increase in narcissism among college students. *Journal of Personality,* 76(4), 919–928.

Twenge, J. M., Liqing, Z., & Im, C. (n.d). It's beyond my control: A cross-temporal meta-analysis of increasing externality in locus of control, 1960–2002. *Personality & Social Psychology Review,* 8(3), 308–319.

Cultivating Character, Purpose, and Moral Identity

Damon, W. (2008). *The Path to Purpose: How Young People Find Their Calling in Life.* New York: Free Press.

Dow, P. (2013). *Virtuous Minds: Intellectual Character Development.* IVP Academic.

Frimer, J. A., & Walker, L. J. (2009). Reconciling the self and morality: An empirical model of moral centrality development. *Developmental Psychology,* 45(6), 1669–1681.

Higgins-D'Alessandro, A., & Power, F. (2005). Character, responsibility, and the moral self. In D. K. Lapsley & F.

Power (Eds.), *Character Psychology and Character Education* (pp. 101–120). Notre Dame, IN: University of Notre Dame Press.

Narvaez, D. (2008). Cultivating morality. *Journal of Moral Education*, 37(4), 539–542.

Peterson, C., & Seligman, M. P. (2004). *Character Strengths and Virtues: A Handbook and Classification*. Washington, DC: American Psychological Association.

Power, F. (2004). The moral self in community. In D. K. Lapsley & D. Narvaez (Eds.), *Moral Development, Self, and Identity* (pp. 47–64). Mahwah, NJ: Lawrence Erlbaum.

Moderating Emotions and Learning through Moderate Challenge

Kagan, J. (2002). *Surprise, uncertainty, and mental structures.* Cambridge, MA US: Harvard University Press.

Turner, J. C., & Meyer, D. K. (2004). A classroom perspective on the principle of moderate challenge in mathematics. *The Journal of Educational Research*, 97(6), 311-318.

Fostering Empathy and Concern for Others

Berger, E. (2008). Caring and character: How close parental bonds foster character development in children. In K. Kline (Ed.), *Authoritative Communities: The Scientific Case for Nurturing the Whole Child* (pp. 355–368). New York: Springer Science + Business Media.

Goodman, T., Greenland, S., & Siegel, D. J. (2012). Mindful parenting as a path to wisdom and compassion. In C. K. Germer & R. D. Siegel (Eds.), *Wisdom and Compassion in Psychotherapy: Deepening Mindfulness in Clinical Practice* (pp. 295–310). New York: Guilford Press.

Hoffman, M. L. (2000). *Empathy and Moral Development:*

Implications for Caring and Justice. New York: Cambridge University Press.

Kline, K. (Ed.) (2008). *Authoritative Communities: The Scientific Case for Nurturing the Whole Child*. New York,: Springer Science + Business Media.

Promoting a Healthy Sense of Self-Worth

Ellis, A. (2013). The value of a human being. In M. E. Bernard (Ed.), *The Strength of Self-Acceptance: Theory, Practice and Research* (pp. 65–72). New York: Springer Science + Business Media.

Heppner, W. L., & Kernis, M. H. (2011). High self-esteem: Multiple forms and their outcomes. In S. J. Schwartz, K. Luyckx, & V. L. Vignoles (Eds.), *Handbook of Identity Theory and Research (vols. 1 and 2)* (pp. 329–355). New York,: Springer Science + Business Media.

Kernis, M. H., & Heppner, W. L. (2008). Individual differences in quiet ego functioning: Authenticity, mindfulness, and secure self-esteem. In H. A. Wayment & J. J. Bauer (Eds.), *Transcending Self-Interest: Psychological Explorations of the Quiet Ego* (pp. 85–93). Washington: American Psychological Association.

Rhodewalt, F. (2006). Possessing and striving for high self-esteem. In M. H. Kernis (Ed.), *Self-Esteem Issues and Answers: A Sourcebook of Current Perspectives* (pp. 281–287). New York: Psychology Press.

Schimel, J., Pyszczynski, T., Arndt, J., & Greenberg, J. (2001). Being accepted for who we are: Evidence that social validation of the intrinsic self reduces general defensiveness. *Journal of Personality & Social Psychology*, 80(1), 35–52.

Thompson, B. L., & Waltz, J. A. (2008). Mindfulness, self-esteem, and unconditional self-acceptance. *Journal of Rational-Emotive & Cognitive Behavior Therapy*, 26(2), 119–126.

Promoting the Growth Mindset, Perseverance, and Emotional Toughness

Duckworth, A. L., Peterson, C., Matthews, M. D., & Kelly, D. R. (2007). Grit: Perseverance and passion for long-term goals. *Journal of Personality & Social Psychology*, 92(6), 1087–1101.

Gunderson, E. A., Gripshover, S. J., Romero, C., Dweck, C. S., Goldin-Meadow, S., & Levine, S. C. (2013). Parent praise to 1- to 3-year-olds predicts children's motivational frameworks 5 years later. *Child Development*, 84(5), 1526–1541.

Li, J. (2012). *Cultural Foundations of Learning: East and West*. New York: Cambridge University Press.

Yeager, D., & Dweck, C. S. (2012). Mindsets that promote resilience: When students believe that personal characteristics can be developed. *Educational Psychologist*, 47(4), 302–314.

The Self-Esteem Myth

Baumeister, R. F., Campbell, J. D., Krueger, J. I., & Vohs, K. D. (2005). Exploding the self-esteem myth. *Scientific American Mind*, 16(4), 50–57.

Hewitt, J. P. (1998). *The Myth of Self-Esteem: Finding Happiness and Solving Problems in America*. New York: Palgrave Macmillan.

Managing Conflict

Brown, S. (2003). *How to Negotiate with Kids even When You Think You Shouldn't*. New York: Penguin Press.

Fisher, R., & Shapiro, D. (2005). *Beyond Reason: Using Emotions as You Negotiate*. New York: Viking.

Fisher, R., Ury, W. L., & Patton, B. (1991). *Getting to Yes:*

Negotiating Agreement without Giving In. New York: Penguin.

Johnson, I. (1997). *Parenting for Prevention: How to Teach Kids to Resolve Conflicts without Violence.* Center City, MN: Hazelden.

Active Listening and Self-Assertion

Burr, W. R. (1990). Beyond I-statements in family communication. *Family Relations, 39*(3), 266–273.

Myers, S. (2000). Empathic listening: Reports on the experience of being heard. *Journal of Humanistic Psychology, 40*(2), 148–173.

Schubert, J. (2007). Engaging youth with the power of listening. *Reclaiming Children & Youth, 15*(4), 227–228.

Helpful Parenting Books

Akin, T., & Palmares, S. (2014). *Anger Control and Conflict Management for Kids: A Learning Guide for the Elementary Grades.* Wellington, FL: Innerchoice.

Berger, E. (1999). *Raising Children with Character: Parents, Trust, and the Development of Personal Integrity.* Lanham, MD: Jason Aronson.

Dweck, C. *Mindset.* New York: Free Press.

Faber, A., & Mazlish, E. (2012). *How to Talk so Kids Will Listen.* New York: Scribner's.

Gordon, T. (1970). *Parent Effectiveness Training.* New York: Wyden.

Gottman, J., & Declaire, J. (1997). *Raising Emotionally Intelligent Children: The Heart of Parenting.* New York: Simon & Schuster.

Kindlon, D. (2001). *Too Much of a Good Thing: Raising Children of Character in an Indulgent Age.* New York: Hyperion.

MacKenzie, R. J. (1998). *Setting Limits: How to Raise Responsible, Independent Children by Providing Clear Boundaries.* New York: Three Rivers Press.

Shure, M. B. (1996). *Raising a Thinking Child: Help Your Young Child Learn to Resolve Everyday Conflicts and Get Along with Others.* New York: Pocket Books.

Shure, M. B. (2000). *Raising a Thinking Child Workbook.* Champaign, IL: Research Press.

Twenge, J. M., & Campbell, W. E. (2009). *The Narcissism Epidemic: Living in the Age of Entitlement.* New York: Atria.

Index

Note: Italicized page locators refer to figures; tables are noted with *t*.